MW00984988

Also by George Singleton

These People Are Us

The Half-Mammals of Dixie

Why Dogs Chase Cars

Novel

Drowning in Gruel

Work Shirts for Madmen

Pep Talks, Warnings, and Screeds

Stray Decorum

Between Wrecks

Calloustown

Staff Picks

You Want More

The Curious Lives of Non-Profit Martyrs

ASIDES

OCCASIONAL ESSAYS ON
DOGS, FOOD, RESTAURANTS, BARS,
HANGOVERS, JOBS, MUSIC, FAMILY TREES,
ROBBERY, RELATIONSHIPS,
BEING BROUGHT UP QUESTIONABLY,
ET CETERA

GEORGE SINGLETON

Asides:

*Occasional Essays on Dogs, Food, Restaurants, Bars, Hangovers,
Jobs, Music, Family Trees, Robbery, Relationships,
Being Brought Up Questionably, Et Cetera*

George Singleton

ESSAYS
ISBN   978-1-958094-29-7

BOOK & COVER DESIGN ❧ EK Larken

AUTHOR PHOTO ❧ Glenda Guion

EastOver Press encourages the use of our publications in educational settings.
For questions about educational discounts, contact us online:
www.EastOverPress.com or info@EastOverPress.com.

PUBLISHED IN THE UNITED STATES OF AMERICA BY

EASTOVER
— PRESS —

ROCHESTER, MASSACHUSETTS
www.EastOverPress.com

ASIDES

GEORGE SINGLETON

For Anyone Mentioned

Contents

Foreword by Abigail Thomas	*13*
Apology/Preface by the author	*15*
Refuse	19
Seven Protective Popeyes	27
Fifth Cousins, Twice Removed	33
I Thank the Church for Teaching Me How to Lie	45
Acting Squirrelly	49
Field Trips for the Unsuspecting	55
The Sex Symbol of the South	61
Back from the Grave	65
Chains	71
Nu-Way Lounge and Restaurant	75
Moon Pie	81
Marking Territory	85
Why I Fear Guns, Butcher Blocks, and Non-Unionized Manual Labor	95
Why We Don't Play Chess	101
The Real Value of Book Reports	107
Gar	115
The Great Singletini	121
An Ode to Hangover Cures	127
How to Write Stories, Lose Weight, Clean up the Environment, and Make $1,000,000	131
The Daily Grind	141
Where I Discovered Narrative Possibilities, Possibly	145
A Fine Restaurant in Nowhere, South Carolina, Run by a Man Named Xue	149
from Writing in a Room that Once Displayed Jesus, Inside a Zoo, Inside a Botanical Garden	159

Why I Write First Drafts by Hand   163
My Writing Mentor   167
Strange Love in a Small Pasture   171
Aristotle and South Carolina   177
Thanksgiving   181

PUBLICATIONS   *189*
ACKNOWLEDGMENTS   *191*
ABOUT THE AUTHOR   *193*

"One place understood helps us understand all places better."

—Eudora Welty

FOREWORD

If you have not had the pleasure of sitting next to George Singleton with a glass of something encouraging in one hand, a bunch of his dogs at your feet, you would do well to get yourself a copy of *Asides*, Singleton's book of essays. It's the next best thing to George in the flesh. Oh boy. You will learn things.

George Singleton is a very funny man. He is also angry, honest, soft hearted, devoted to his animals and his friends. He attributes his having become a writer to barbecue, and to having driven a garbage truck, both of which arguments are convincing. He could write about a Tootsie Roll and keep me reading.

He can enter a room, breathe in the air, breathe out a story.

Ever heard of Elmer Fudpucker, Sr.? Sex Symbol of the South? Didn't think so. Well, in the course of explaining the presence of this man in his life, Singleton mentions a song called "Meat Man" which Jerry Lee Lewis sang. Dear God, there is no word in English to describe how brilliantly terrible it is. And when Singleton issues the following command: "Go listen to 'Meat Man' and come back here." I did. Then I did it again. Then I made my kids listen. It is my new addiction. I had forgotten what a genius Jerry Lee Lewis was. Thank you, George.

Speaking of addiction, you might find Singleton's cure for hangovers useful, at least for a shudder and a laugh. His advice on beginning to write is more helpful and involves picking up trash.

He doesn't like racists. He once loved a band called Moon Pie which should have made it big. He had a job as a lifeguard although he didn't know how to swim. (Nobody drowned.)

He can move you to tears from time to time, and if it is over a fat black pig whose best friend was a horse who died, you will find yourself scrounging around for Kleenex.

George doesn't suffer fools gladly or otherwise, but I have a feeling that if you showed up on all fours in George's yard looking like hell he would probably adopt you. Come to think of it, that's not such a bad idea.

— ABIGAIL THOMAS, author of
A Three Dog Life and *Safekeeping*

Apology / Preface

I hate writing essays. It's not my gig. Oh, I'll write short stories like a crazed SOB, on and on, but I hate writing essays. First off, I'm not smart enough. It feels as though I'm writing some kind of student essay. I don't have anything to say. I walk around most days going *doh-dee-doh-dee-doh.* I nod at people left and right, say, "Hey, how're you doing?" and they look at me going, fine, fine, fine, in the canned fruits aisle.

There are plenty of other writers who can rightly espouse their views on politics, sexual predicaments, cooking, weather, football head injuries, hairstyles, music, cats, movie reviews, book reviews, spousal problems, baseball, gun control, melanoma, and global warning. AM radio, social media, suicide, gas prices, grocery stores, Dolly Parton, George Jones v. Merle Haggard, how students need to play recorders and finger paint more often. College football players getting paid for their visages, pro basketball players dealing with technicals, Kentucky politicians dealing with sane voters throwing bottles of pee at their rooftops, eighteen-year-old kids buying AR-15s and taking them inside elementary schools, idiot Kentucky/Tennessee/South Carolina politicians taking up for the AR-15 kid, family members who turn into hoarders. Drugs, questionable doctors, questionable funeral home directors, questionable preachers, questionable teachers, questionable veterinarians, questionable coaches, questionable used car dealers, questionable police officers, questionable butchers, questionable organic farmers, questionable massage therapists. On and on. There happen to be some great essayists. I don't count myself in this group.

The weather! Professional baseball! Music! Who is better, Flannery O'Connor or Eudora Welty? Faulkner or Hemingway? Pynchon or Barth? Green Giant or Bird's Eye? The more I think about how little I know, the more I understand how I need to shy away from the world of nonfiction.

Evidently there are questionable editors, too, because most of the previously published essays in this book started off because an editor wrote or called, said something like, "You got anything about your dogs?" or "What's a good hangover remedy?" or "Ever had a crazy ending to a relationship?" I sat down and wrote all of them in the same way I wrote a term paper about Upton Sinclair's *The Jungle* back in the eleventh grade — tight-jawed, white-knuckled, cringing, worried that I'd massacre the use of "lay" and "lie."

One day in April 2022, with zero ideas for a new short story, I thought to myself, "I ought to collect all my old essays from the last twenty or thirty years." I'd been reading a couple collections of fine essays. I got inside the innards of this computer and found out that, oddly enough, I'd saved none of my nonfiction pieces. On top of that, I'd only kept a couple of the magazines, and none of the books in which they'd appeared originally. I think I found three online. I know for a fact I wrote an essay about a wake of black buzzards who live across from my house, but I never could find the piece. So, here are the ones I found, in no particular order. I need to thank various editors for prodding me. I changed some of them a minuscule bit. I wrote a few more—ones I thought necessary about my upbringing, more or less, just so the book wasn't the length of a menu.

Maybe in another twenty or thirty years I'll have another clutch of nonfiction pieces. I know, now, to save them, because re-typing isn't exactly my favorite thing to do.

— GS

REFUSE

'M PRETTY SURE my blind headfirst leap into writing fiction occurred for the same reasons it occurred with my brethren: I had discovered some new types of music, I'd been scorned one too many times by a woman, and my summer job involved driving a garbage truck. I'm no expert in astronomy or anthropology, but it seems plausible and likely that the alignment of Tom Waits and The Clash, of "Get lost, I hate you," and "You gone have to drive the garbage truck that don't have no power steering," said by a man named Lonnie, will only result in a kid spending late-night hours with pen to paper, trying to be as existential as possible. I'm not so sure that I've ever thanked any type of Supreme Being for the Summer of 1978. Maybe I shouldn't.

It doesn't matter about how I went from listening to Grateful Dead to either punk or cry-in-your-beer narratives bellowed out by a gravelly-voiced seer. And I certainly understand now why a college girl would think to herself, *Man, what was I thinking when I started dating this guy?* No, what had the most impact was the summer job, which started off as my needing only to drive a special flatbed truck with a giant forklift on back instead of the bed. This was for the city of Greenwood, South Carolina, my hometown.

In the previous summers, since the age of fifteen, I had driven dump trucks and water trucks, working for the "beautification committee." I had cleaned up flowerbeds around town, watered the plants, spread pine straw, and that sort of thing. I hoed around the town fountain, dipping the hoe into water when I saw quarters. I spread mulch, and dug ditches, and pretended I knew what I was doing. I'd spent hours trickling water from a fire hydrant into the truck's reservoir so I could take a nap in the shade. I'd driven the dump truck (which you could get going about forty miles an hour, turn off the ignition, then turn it back on in order to make the truck backfire) with my coworkers—college kids—to Lake Greenwood, to gather up pine straw from one of the summer-job workers' parents' lake house. We'd buy beer at this little store along the way, load up the truck in about five minutes, go swimming and fishing, drinking beer, then drive back just before lunch. After lunch we'd unload the pine straw and make a second pilgrimage to the lake house, et cetera.

I don't want to tattle on everyone involved, but Charlie, Phillip, Eddie, and Scurry—what a name, Scurry!—all ended up being productive, non-criminal citizens, from what I understand. For some reason none of them chose to write, or quit early on like rational beings should. They listened to regular music and had steady girl-friends who liked to dance, I imagine.

Anyway, for some reason the bosses deemed me responsible enough, finally, in the summer of my junior year in college, to promote me to the Sanitation Department. Originally, I was in charge of washing out Dempsey Dumpsters with a steam hose of sorts, then painting the insides with a brown de-ruster. I painted the outsides green with a roller and, more often than not, signed my name somewhere on the inside. It was my job to drive to the dumpsters with the flatbed truck with the forklift on the back, pick up the bin, and bring it to the shop area. Sometime in the middle of the night these dumpsters had been emptied by the third-shift driver, a man named Fletcher. What a sweet job he had, with no one named Lonnie to yell at him.

I should mention this: There are people who work at department stores and pharmacies and such who steal from their employers. I know it's hard to believe. But on occasion, I would drive my fancy forklift-in-the-bed truck to a Dempsey Dumpster, lift the lid, and learn that the bin wasn't empty. Did Fletcher forget part of his route last night? I would wonder immediately. Then I would notice how there didn't seem to be actual trash in the dumpster. No, somebody had placed perfectly good, say, albums, clothes, hair dryers, cigarettes, boxes of Russell Stover candy (which melt in a dumpster, by the way), candlesticks, candles (they melt, too), pipe tobacco, pipes, belts, sandals, and a Velcro-type dart game into the dumpster. Could it be that an employee of Eckerd's Drugs, or Belk, planned to come back after work and take what he or she had placed in my Dempsey Dumpster? Could it be I should take said items, in order to make the employee understand that life isn't fair, just like it's not fair in the world of American fiction, of which I wanted to be a part?

So there was that wonderful part of the job. This "stealing from the thieves" part of my job, I feel sure now, had some kind of effect on my writerly beginnings. But it wasn't enough.

Again, I'm no anthropologist, but surely some scholar has delved into the world of typical work weeks and noticed how many sanitation department workers don't show up on Mondays. So was the case in the summer of 1978. Hangovers and knifings and jail time seemed to be the prevalent reasons. One early morning Lonnie came to me and said, "We ain't got no drivers this morning, two in jail, fellow stabbed Leon, ain't enough licenses. You drive one of the trucks?"

Lonnie had a head like a bowling ball. His eyes bugged out and his mouth never closed. Lonnie kept his head shaved way before it was fashionable. He yelled at everyone constantly, except for a barrel-chested, long-haired white garbage truck driver named Henry who came back to the shop after his route and practiced shooting his high-tech bow and arrow at a target placed right beside where I steam-cleaned dumpsters.

I had already declared my philosophy major in college, so I didn't know enough not to say, "'Ain't got no drivers' is a double negative. Do you mean?..."

I think he actually pulled me by the ear, up the slight hill to where the trucks were parked.

My co-workers on these Mondays, and then usually Tuesdays and Wednesdays, were named Honeypie and Esby. Because one of the newer trucks was always in for repair, I had to drive a garbage truck manufactured circa 1965 that didn't have power steering. Listen, when it was heavy with what my townspeople discarded daily, I had to get the thing going about thirty miles an hour before I could turn the wheel.

Again, this particular truck was used only when no other was available. I got in, Honeypie and Esby jumped in the front seat with me for the ride to our route's first can. Honeypie said, "Something stink."

It was a fucking garbage truck, I thought. Cause and effect! Philosophy 101.

Honeypie reached beneath my seat, between my legs. He pulled out a grease-stained brown paper bag and extracted a tin foil-covered meatloaf sandwich that had been there since the last time this truck saw use. Let's say it had been two weeks. I don't know what the gestation period is for the types of flies that hang out at sanitation department yards, but that rancid meatloaf sandwich had enough maggots squirming between bread and beef for an entire hospital wing of patients with necrotic tissue in need of clean-up.

"Summody wasted a good sandwich," Esby said. "Who don't eat they lunch, who don't eat they lunch?"

It was Monday. Maybe I, too, had a hangover. I opened the door, sick to my stomach.

Oddly, this is the first time — thirty-one years later — that I've written about driving a garbage truck. All in all it may have been my best job ever. I got paid a couple bucks more than minimum wage. If we finished routes at one or two o'clock, we were done for the day and paid eight hours' worth of work. If I had understood how America's obsession with junk and antiques would occur years later, I would be a millionaire, for Honeypie and Esby probably threw Tiffany lamps and Chippendale chairs and antique Royal typewriters into the back of the truck. I worked my shift, I returned to my parents' house, and I wrote fiction that concerned characters living in New York and Paris—places I had never visited at the time—who worked as doctors and lawyers—things I would never do or really care to know about.

When there were enough drivers for the trucks, I returned to picking up dumpsters and cleaning them. Filled with the anticipation of finding a dishonorable and disgruntled employee's stolen goods, I drove to my sites—the same feeling I get nowadays when writing a story. When there were zero nearly-stolen products hidden away, I felt deflated—the same feeling today when I get a rejection in the mail. The highs and lows of sanitation work, baby, are the same highs and lows of writing daily.

Only later did I understand perhaps Honeypie and Esby didn't see their occupations as the best jobs ever created. Honeypie said more than once, "Sheet, I'mo kill Lonnie and get me a guh goddamn job."

More than once Esby said, "Bitch don't realize I working my ass off while she down on Waller Skreet drinking beer." Waller Street— aptly named—was a short alley off Main that held three or four juke joints. Back in previous summers, I'd driven my dump truck down there too fast, turned off the ignition, and watched the windows shake to my backfire.

They never looked me in the face when they spoke. One time Esby was in the truck's trough in back, riding to the next stop, when I heard him yelling, then in my side mirror saw him running in the road. A rat had crawled onto his lap, and he jumped. When there were narrow driveways or alleys with cans far away, they asked me to back my way right up to the cans, which took much longer than their walking to the garbage and bringing it back. I think it was their way of saying, "This isn't supposed to be an easy life, boy." I think it might've been their way of saying, "Remember these days when we're still here and you out of college, with a good job, like roofing, or painting houses, still a decade away from ever having a story published."

And then there's this: One day with Honeypie and Esby, we idled in line at the county dump. They sat up front with me. Esby kept yelling, "Hurry up, man, I gots to get me home." In a non-power steering garbage truck, one needs to back in line, then drive as fast as possible toward the man with the bulldozer once the previous truck exits the area. At the last second, one turns the wheel hard to the right, in order to eventually back up toward where the garbage truck's contents should be discharged.

Honeypie hummed. He said, "I ain't looking," but I didn't know why.

Esby said, "It ain't right. Gone happen to us one day."

"That man ain't got no soul, do what he do."

I thought they were, perhaps, hallucinating, or had been reading Faulkner and were in stream-of-consciousness mode.

This man named Dalton, who worked as the dogcatcher and whom I called Dalton the Dogcatcher, had been in his pickup truck right before me in line. He'd shoved what appeared to be a refrigerator box. He drove away and looked at me—college boy—with his beady little eyes. I looked in the rearview mirror as the county dump's bulldozer man shoved the box further up a heap. The box split open, and I saw probably ten stiff dogs emerge, legs out, eyes like sad peeled muscadines. I don't think, at the time, I thought about how those poor strays would be buried in what trash I was about to dump. I didn't think about how Esby and Honeypie might've felt their lives were on about the same course as a stray dog's, but I do now.

SEVEN PROTECTIVE POPEYES

ALWAYS FELT deep down my odd assortment of ex-strays all hailed from the "Me" generation.

Oh, I brought them each into the fold like they were down-on-their luck drifters, and knew they didn't carry "Will Fetch for Food" cardboard signs only because they didn't possess opposable thumbs and Magic Markers. And at first each dog pretty much retained a look in the eyes similar to that of the planet's terrified, hungry, orphaned children. They—whether ten or eighty pounds, whether appearing biracial or a mixture of forty breeds—continued the ruse for a week, then felt comfortable enough, evidently, to join the pack under its inherent, "Me First" banner.

My dogs' tendencies became apparent this past November when I realized they didn't care whatsoever about my undergoing pains and side effects of possible *E. coli* infection. There'd been a massive recall of all bagged spinach, and every grocery store in America sent produce managers on an endless beeline between their vegetable stations and the Dumpster out back. The *E. coli* outbreak had killed a few people scattered

27

across the country, and left other healthy-eating individuals somewhere between painful gastrointestinal episodes and outright kidney failure. A panic ensued, of course. *Terrorists had struck our food supply!* some survivalists declared, as did a few of the more paranoid members of Congress.

Let me say right now I have never been known as a "healthy eater" in regard to the recommended fifty-six daily portions of fruits and vegetables. That's another story. But for some reason, I couldn't fathom not eating spinach if and when I wanted the stuff. So I got out one of the garden books I rarely open, and learned that, indeed, spinach is a fall crop. So is broccoli. Up until this point, I'd only planted tomatoes (which my dogs took off the vine, thinking that tennis balls had ripened), cucumbers (which my dogs picked and carried around like giant green cigars, maybe in hopes of being in the next C.M. Coolidge portrait of dogs playing poker), squash (which my dogs seemed to use as juggling clubs), and so on. They never touched the jalapeños, but then again I don't have any Chihuahua-mix strays.

I got to work. I bought topsoil. During the last week in September, I constructed a raised-bed garden that measured 8x24 feet. Spinach seeds cost only ninety-five cents an ounce, as it turned out, and there were about a million seeds in an ounce. I planted eight rows. Off to the side I planted a dozen broccoli plants, just in case the terrorists struck that lovely plant next. I watered every morning and tried not to pay attention to my dogs sitting in a row behind me, staring. *I hope he's planting something that attracts moles, voles, and shrews that we can dig up and roll on,* I could almost read on Maggie's and Hershey's faces. Charlie, Marty, and Stella looked as if they wanted Brussels sprouts, of all things, seeing as they would fit their smaller mouths as compared to tomato/tennis balls. Nick and Dooley, kind-of-black-Lab and kind-of-Pointer, respectively, wanted something to attract more slow-moving doves.

I came back inside all smiles each morning from tending the garden. Tell me I can't eat spinach when I want to eat spinach, I thought. I took each of my seven dogs aside and said, "You're in charge of making sure no one else digs in the garden. You're in charge of keeping the other dogs from using the new raised-bed garden as a gigantic Porta Potti. That would kind of defeat the anti-*E. coli* purpose of this little experiment."

Every one of my dogs nodded. They promised.

In late October, I had to leave for five weeks in order to be some kind of writer-in-residence at an MFA program in Wilmington, North Carolina. Every other writer in the United States must've been busy for a month; perhaps they didn't want to travel around with possible spinach terrorists in their midst, I don't know. I left on October 24. My spinach had come up nicely, in straight rows, maybe an inch high. I thought, *When I come back I'll have to pick the stuff, blanch it, get it into freezer bags quickly.* I had read up on that part of the operation soon after the gardening book, understand.

About ten days into my residency, I drove home feeling guilty for leaving my patient better half, Glenda, with seven dogs to take care of. She couldn't leave her job—oh, I should mention this Wilmington gig included a house on Wrightsville Beach—and she wasn't exactly ecstatic I had to work nonstop for three hours on Mondays, spend a day reading student work sometime during the week, and use the rest of my time there to make friends with seagulls.

I came in the side door to our house, and the indoor dogs leapt on me as they always did. They didn't make eye contact as usual, though. When I let them outside with me—I wanted to go check on the garden, seeing as we'd undergone a dry stretch of weather—they took off immediately for the back corner of the property. They passed Maggie and Hershey along the way, two obviously sated dogs who barely moved from their spots in the sun. I called back to Glenda, "What the hell happened to the spinach?" My dog-members of the Me Generation took up their posts in the garden, growling at one another. *This is my spinach, this is my spinach, this is my spinach,* and grazing on it at will. *I will be Popeye, I will be Popeye, I will be Popeye.* They acted the same way they did over a rock, or a dried-up miniature peach that finally fell off one of the trees like a scab, or a scrap of paper that had flown into the yard. I might've cursed loudly. I could hear children being herded in from miles around, could hear drapes and Venetian blinds being closed, could sense the slight populace of Pickens County dialing 911. Marty and Nick got to their claims first, slowly walked over to the tallest broccoli plant, and lifted their legs. The other five dogs followed.

I took Dooley with me back to Wrightsville Beach. He, too, showed interest in the seagulls. It seemed like he spent a great deal of time looking for vegetation in order to do his business, and the waves coming in only confused him. Other dogs being walked around on leashes didn't fascinate him, and I wondered if he grew homesick for his pack of selfish buddies. Most every dawn, and at midday, and again at night, I walked him out to the beach path, where he sniffed every stalk of sea oats, then pulled me back to the house. He showed no interest in the rawhide chews I bought.

So when my teaching gig finished, I packed up and started the six-hour drive home. Dooley sat in the passenger seat, per usual, staring straight ahead. He didn't bark at cows or horses, and when I stopped at South of the Border on I-95 so he could check out the giant sculptures of giraffes, gorillas, and rhinos, he looked at me as if to say, *Let's not waste our time; let's get home as soon as possible.*

He whined and wagged his tail when I turned onto Hester Store Road, a mile away. We got out of the Jeep, but he didn't run to the side door where we normally entered. No, he took off—maybe he's part Pointer and part Greyhound—straight for the spinach. He sniffed every remaining leaf in each row, then got down on the ground as close to the spinach as possible, as if waiting for his buddies to come outside so he could tell stories, so he could listen to them tell their tales of Bluto coming by.

FIFTH COUSINS,
TWICE REMOVED

S IGNING UP FOR Ancestry.com has never been one of my priorities. Call me selfish, or one who finds no reason to know he's related to Napoleon, Joan d'Arc, or Charlemagne. Understand I know how this might make me sound conceited, uncaring, solipsistic, self-absorbed, and so on. Maybe I possess some kind of uber-intuitiveness, and I don't want to know the ins-and-outs of my ancestors. Some people I know love to regale in stories about their family trees: of philanthropists, do-gooders, cancer-researchers, governors, kings, military geniuses, and track stars. Fine. Good for them. I don't want to stand around some kind of cocktail party—as if we have cocktail parties in South Carolina—and feel pressure to tell the truth: mental institution patient, prisoner, draft dodger, philanderer, swindler, pinhooker, snake oil salesperson, prostitute, crank, unfulfilled writer/artist/gambler. This will come off as either short-sighted or mean, but I have zero tolerance for people who puff themselves up because they're related to Sister Teresa when they have done—in my estimation—nothing to further the cause. I want to say to them, "Go pick up roadside litter on Saturdays" or "Do you read to blind orphans on a weekly basis?" or "How many dogs have you rescued from the Humane Society?"

Not that I've done those things, for the most part—I've never read to blind orphans—but I don't go around bragging about being related to Gandhi, either.

One summer, as I wasn't teaching, I got an email from the senior director of marketing at the college where I worked. She wrote to me, "The email below was sent to our general 'marketing' email address. Thought you'd get a kick out it, and may even want to respond to her."

Of course I thought right away, *This is going to be about reading some rich guy's manuscript.* Or, *Some eighty-year-old alumnus is complaining about something I wrote. Somebody wants me to come speak to the Kiwanis/Lion's/ Rotary/Chamber of Commerce monthly meeting.* I'd been asked to do so in the past. What were they thinking? They wanted some kind of motivational speaker. I've never been asked back.

Nope. Here's what I got:

> Mr. Singleton had a great-grandfather, a dentist named Marcus Gibson Vaughan, who was killed by an officer while attempting to burglarize a store in order to buy Christmas presents for his children in 1932 Georgia. I'm wondering if he has written anything about this incident.

No "To Whom It May Concern." No

"Dear Director of Marketing." No "Dear Sir or Madam." No "I can't figure out how to send this to the President, the Provost, the Dean, or the Chairperson of the English Department."

I'd never heard this story. I knew about my Aunt Martha, who had some kind of lobotomy performed by Dr. Thigpen — *The Three Faces of Eve* Thigpen — back in the day. I knew how my paternal grandmother played honky-tonk piano in a burlesque-type bar owned by Jack Ruby in Dallas, Texas, the same Jack Ruby who killed Lee Harvey Oswald, who killed JFK. One time I met a JFK conspiracy theorist who told me my grandmother showed up in the Warren Report, but I don't know if that's true.

I knew about a cousin who got caught selling heroin back in the sixties, about a gay cousin who went to prison, got out, couldn't take it anymore, and killed himself. I knew about a cousin who went to prison for somehow stealing money from the National Guard, and got sent to prison.

My own father's belly exploded full of pus in 1960, and it ended up being cancer. He spent eighteen months in and out of a San Francisco hospital. He got overexposed to radiation, got burned to a crisp — these rectangular, maroon four-by-six inch squares that seared from belly-through-back — and he returned to a merchant ship, then ended up falling forty-five feet into the hold of a ship: I knew how the Sailors Union of the Pacific's lawyers contended that the ladder didn't falter during a storm up the west coast between Long Beach and Washington state, but my dad intentionally jumped in a suicidal attempt which ended with fifty-seven broken bones (two hips, both knees, about every rib, femurs, metatarsi, count them up). I knew how my father went from morphine addict to Darvon and Phenobarbital addict, to one-quart-of-vodka-a-day addict, to a series of artificial hip operations. When one one-and-thirteen-sixteenths-inch Zimaloy metal hip went out, they put in another. I have the old ones here on my desk.

And, of course, I knew about my own discrepancies.

Here are a couple stories I know for true and remember: In the summer of 1965, my father, "disabled," because of the forty-five-foot fall, drove my mother and me to South Carolina, where his father now lived. Back in the day my grandfather lived in Dallas, with his wife, Nelta. Nelta's the one who played piano for Jack Ruby. Nelta had a father named Marcus Vaughan.

On the drive between Anaheim, California and Greenwood, South Carolina—this was 1965—we stopped by Dallas so my father could introduce me to his mother, a woman who played the piano, and so on. This was July. I remember it being hot. I had just turned seven years old. Here, and I swear it's true: "Little George, the Easter Bunny left you something."

My paternal grandmother, Nelta—comrade of murderer Jack Ruby—handed over one of those cellophane-covered boxes with a chocolate bunny inside. July. The bunny had turned white. She'd gnawed off the head already. She handed me a stale, white, headless chocolate bunny.

My father walked on crutches at this time, he hit me on my hamstrings—pop!—and said,

"What do you say, son?"

I started crying. I said, "Thanks."

"Thanks, what?" he said.

I don't want to say anything bad about my paternal grandmother—the woman whose father tried to burglarize a store in 1932—but this all occurred in an apartment in Dallas, Texas, in the summer. The place owned no air-conditioning. She wore a fur stole. Her hair wasn't of a natural color. Now that I think about it, I guess she did come off as the daughter of a criminal.

I said, "Grandma."

A woman named Diane Bender wrote my college's director of marketing. She'd included her email address. What else could I do but write back to her, "I've never heard this story that you found necessary to tell the marketing department. Do you think I should be reprimanded for having such a supposed relative?"

Goddamn, I'm serious: I completely understand someone writing, "I thought you should know that ---- had been convicted of screwing a goat," or whatever, but why should I be blamed for people in my past bloodstream?

I wrote back to her, "I just want to know why you didn't plain contact me, instead of my employer. It seems odd. Are we related? How did you know I'm a writer? What got you on this Vaughan track? This dentist Vaughan was my biological grandma's dad. I've never heard this story, and only met her once, when I was seven."

Here's what I got back:

To be honest, I didn't have the nerve to contact you. I hoped the person I emailed would refer me to a librarian or other person knowledgeable about your work. It seemed that a story about poor Dr. Vaughan and the impact of his misguided actions would have made an interesting Southern story, so I thought that you might already have written one. I feel privileged that you responded to me directly. You and I are fifth cousins twice removed. In my genealogy work I bring forward as many lines as possible so that I can sort out my DNA matches. Your Vaughan line descends in part from a man named John Shepard, who died in 1806 Georgia. From obituaries and so forth, I was led to a biosketch of you in your induction into the Fellowship of Southern Writers. I'm impressed by writers who publish. I've been writing a novel about my mother's early Texas ancestors for 30 years and have only 125 pages...The story about Nelta Vaughan is probably true. Her obituary had the phrase 'singer and pianist in numerous Dallas clubs and restaurants,' some of which must certainly have been owned by Ruby.

I wrote Diane back. How in the world did my mean reputation get all the way to a woman I never met—how people didn't have "the nerve" to contact me? What else could I do for a fifth cousin twice-removed? How could I not cotton to a woman who, unknowingly, found herself committed to a white-trash fifth cousin twice removed, whatever that meant? Poor, sad, Diane, always searching for people way more influential and popular and meaningful than my picayune self:

Hey Diane—
Thanks, Cuz. To be honest, I come from a long-line of ne'er-do-wells. Lots of ex-convicts on that side of my father's family, it seems, and drunks. I didn't fall far from the tree, obviously. Somewhere along that line you might come across a woman who owned a boarding house in Columbia, SC—I think her name might've been Janie—who catered solely, it seems, to young men at a barber college. I met her once. Strange woman—though I was a kid, so maybe everyone seemed weird. Also, my Aunt Martha—this would be Nelta Vaughan Sistrunk's daughter, one of my dad's sisters—underwent some kind of brain surgery performed by Dr. Thigpen, in Augusta, GA. He's the guy who worked with that *Three Faces of Eve* woman. One time my other aunt—Bettye—called from Texas to say she had gone blind. Then she went on to talk about how she drove to the eye doctor's office, and so on. My mom said, "You drove blind?" Aunt Bettye's response was, "Oh, I know the route by heart."

Like I said, there's a reason why I never found myself attracted to finding out more. I figured this was a done deal (I made four Cs in Algebra I, and three Cs and one B in Algebra II — Ms. Brannon actually kissed me on the lips, in front of the class, when I made that fourth nine-weeks B) so don't ask me about the math of cousins and removal. But fifth cousin twice-removed Diane Bender sent a few photos of newspaper articles. The one from the *Atlanta Constitution*, dated December 22, 1932, had a sub-title that goes, "Dr. M. G. Vaughan, in Dying Statement, Said He Was Seeking Christmas Gift for Daughter, Marshall Declares." "Augusta Dentist Shot Dead in Attempt at Burglary" happened to be the headline. Right there on the front page of the newspaper, too, it listed out Marcus Vaughan, DDS's living relatives: Mrs. Harold Heard, Mrs. Paul Crowder, Miss Virginia Vaughan, Miss Vivian Vaughan, a son named Mr. M.G. Vaughan, and, of course, Mrs. George Singleton.

Again, I'm no math whiz, but my father was born in 1925. His mom, Nelta, had to be at least thirty in 1932, my father seven. I wrote to Diane, somewhere in there, how it might not be my relatives, et cetera. Why would this dentist be needing to buy gifts for his already-grown-up daughter who lived in Dallas?

And I thought to myself, I had a relative who was a dentist? A dentist! Man, I'm special. Some people are related to earls and dukes, but I got me a dentist somewhere in my family tree!

Diane sent me attachments from the *Daily-Times* in Burlington, North Carolina, with the headline "Dentist Loses Life in 'Santa Claus Holdup," and another from the *Asheville Citizen-Times* that declared "Augusta Dentist, Turned

Burglar, Shot By Officer." All of the stories mentioned how my great-grandfather hatched this idea with three other companions, and that my great grandfather wished to have money to buy gifts for his "visiting" daughter. The men arrested—my great grandfather ended up the only man shot and killed by Marshall R.S. Adams —had broken into a Watson Brothers store. The article in the Burlington paper mentioned how, "He had never given us any trouble before." Earlier in the same article the paper published "he participated in teh affair because he was desperately in need of money to finance the holiday visit of his children."

That's a quote. Teh. Not "the," Teh. That's from the paper. Teh. So maybe I can label this Fake News.

She sent along, too, a photocopy of the death certificate. My great-grandfather was fifty-six years old. He happened to be a widower.

Why had my father never mentioned this entire story to me? Jesus Christ, I knew all the other stories: I knew how my father once got knocked out by, in a special Army-related boxing match with, Rocky Graziano. I knew about how one time a college-educated boatswain kept yelling at my father to load up lumber, that my father yelled down from the crane for the guy to move his hands—this involved a large pallet of lumber, a dock, some steel cables, and a man with his hands holding said cables—the man didn't, and my father pulled up a lever that, eventually, lopped off the college boy's thumbs.

He felt it needful to educate me on a relative who spent time in Milledgeville and Columbia mental institutions, the ones who lived in prisons, his good friend who got arrested and imprisoned for manufacturing fake casino chips out in Nevada.

One time I came home from high school to find my mother crying in her chair. I asked what the problem was, and she said Dad might be going to jail. Then Dad came home whistling, a big smile on his face. It seems that he hired out a down-on-his-luck carpenter, told the man to charge supplies at Snead's Lumber, and my father got a bill a month later that included a new circular saw, drill, and so on. My father found the guy seated on a bar stool at the Sunken Gardens Lounge (on land which now holds a Fatz Cafe, unfortunately). Dad confronted the guy, who said, "Go to hell, Crip," because of my father's limp.

They say this guy actually lifted off the bar-stool and onto the counter when my father's uppercut broke the man's jaw. No charges were filed. My father took me to the hospital to visit the carpenter, oddly enough.

I knew about my father rolling his VW Bug on a narrow two-lane, drunk with his friend Herbert the wannabe-country-star. I'd witnessed three-day parties from the safety of our basement. I knew how my step-grandmother had been married something like seven times, the first to a shepherd in Walla Walla, Washington.

Listen, I had an aunt who gave birth to a child out of wedlock, married another man soon thereafter, and — although everyone on my

mother's side of the family knew this story —
no one ever told my cousin Jim. I happened to
find Jim's birth certificate, in a safe, back when
I was in college. "Father Unknown" was clearly
typed out. My cousin Jim only figured it out at
his father's funeral, when some well-meaning
mourner got up to tell a story about my Uncle
Alex, and somehow let it slip that he was the
best father ever, even though ...

Just know I could list about a hundred of
these people and incidents and situations. If I
did one thing as an only child in South Carolina,
I listened.

But nothing — nothing — about a store-
robbing dentist great-grandfather.

My father died in 1983 at the age of fifty-
seven. My mother passed away in 2015 at the age
of eighty-seven. Had Diane Bender contacted
the director of marketing just a few years earlier,
maybe I could've gotten the scoop on this.

And what else do I not know? I tell you what
I do know: I don't want to know. I know enough.
So Ancestry.com can send me unsolicited emails
all it wants, but I'm not biting. Yet.

An aside: When we moved to South Carolina,
my father thought it necessary for me to get a
pet white rabbit. I remember that day. He said,
"What you need is a pet rabbit!"

I said, "What?" I'd never mentioned how I
wanted a rabbit. We had a poodle, a toy poodle,
named Cuddles. Yeah, go ahead and make fun
of me.

"Come on," my father said, and he drove me
out into the country where this one-armed man
named Mr. Dilleshaw sold rabbits. One time I

saw a documentary called *Pets or Meat,* about rabbits being sold, and I thought about this one-armed guy. I thought about Cuddles, too, if it matters.

I picked out an albino rabbit and named it Snowball. Singletons aren't known for their creativity. My father said, "Shake hands with Mr. Dilleshaw." As it ended up, Mr. Dilleshaw didn't have a right arm. I stuck out my right hand, and he took it with his left, kind of like shaking hands with, I don't know, Senator Bob Dole.

My father popped me on my hamstrings with his right crutch when we walked back to the car, as I held Snowball. He said, "Boy, you got to pay attention."

Snowball died about two months later, in the unused fireplace of the house my parents rented. No one's ever written any of my employers about this situation.

Aside: My father worked at his father's textile supply company for about a year, then got fired for walking out of a church service. It took a while, but my father started up a business to compete with his own father, though it was in my mother's name, what with the disability checks coming in. In the seventh grade, my grandfather showed up at my junior high school and tried to kidnap me. Let's put that up on the family tree.

I THANK THE CHURCH FOR
TEACHING ME HOW TO LIE

INEVER ATTENDED church until I'd turned seven years old in Greenwood, South Carolina. My father knew the Bible front and back, brought up Baptist in Dallas. My mother attended a Methodist church in Muskegon, Michigan. I have no clue why I didn't go to church from ages birth until seven. Hell, I wasn't even baptized.

But when we moved to South Carolina so my disabled father could get paid under the table by his father, someone thought it necessary for us to attend Callie Self Baptist Church, in the middle of the Mathews Mill Village. We went Sunday/Wednesday night, Sunday/Wednesday night, Sunday/Wednesday night. I remember having to go to a Sunday school service and outright crying because I didn't know who the hell Jesus was—we had coloring books handed out, and all the other kids seemed to know of this mysterious man who wore, what I considered, a dress.

Sunday/Wednesday, Sunday/Wednesday, and so on. This didn't last a year. It was 1965. The Civil Rights Movement churned in all other parts of the country. On one of these Wednesday nights, the preacher decided to open up the floor to any questions from the congregation. I wore a seersucker coat; I remember this much. My hair stayed in a buzz cut, with a little tag of longer hair — maybe an inch — in front. It was kind of a backwards rat tail, if said rat got its tail snapped off in a trap.

I don't remember anything else about this — I don't remember anything about going to church, except for crying when I didn't know the significance or identification of Christ. No sermons or hymns remain in my memory. I kind of remember a bunch of men, wearing suits and ties, standing out in front of the church afterwards, smoking cigarettes, talking mill business. Looking back, it seemed more of a bi-weekly networking extravaganza as opposed to a session that involved the Golden Rule.

"Any y'all have a question?" the preacher said in a high-whining voice.

One man stood up and said, "What are we supposed to do if a Black man shows up here?" Except he didn't use the term "Black man."

Another man stood up and yelled out, "Ignore him, and hope he don't come back."

I remember lots of laughter in the room. Har har har. Nodding heads, slapped knees.

My father got up, letting out a grunt. He had his crutches pointed askew. I don't think he said, "Come on," or "That's enough," or "I'm only getting up because my broken hips hurt real bad." This was before his first successful artificial hip operation. At this point, he plain had nails banged into his bones trying to keep things in place, and one of his shoes had a sole and heel about two inches thicker than the other.

He pulled me up, and I thought I'd done

something wrong. My mother stood. We walked out—and we hadn't sat in the very back of the vestibule or anything, no, we were near the front—and my father's crutches squeaked. We exited the church at about .25 mph. He had those metal crutches with arm bands—I keep them hanging on the wall where I write now—and they could've used a couple big WD-40 squirts, if WD-40 became available in South Carolina at the time.

We left. We skedaddled. My father cussed the entire drive home: "Goddamn son-of-a-bitch racists."

From that point on, I wasn't allowed to attend church. Later, if I had a nice girlfriend who went to church like everyone else did in Greenwood, and if she said to me something like, "Will you go to church with me?" or—I had a Catholic girlfriend once—"Will you go to midnight mass?" I'd say something to my dad, and he'd say, "Nope."

When I ended up going to Furman University—at the time Baptist-affiliated—he said, "Good for you. I ain't paying any money to a Baptist college. Figure it out, if you want to go there."

I got work study. I had some money saved up. It cost me nothing to apply, because good track coach Coach Keesling rigged something. I went, knowing I'd be a little different there. I knew I'd tell some lies, just like I did throughout elementary, junior, and high school when someone said, "Where you go to church?"

I have the church to thank in regard to teaching me how to lie, I guess.

ACTING SQUIRRELLY

WE'RE DOWN TO three and one-eighths dogs, plus the tailless cat. So that's three and one-eighths dog, and seven-eighths of a cat. The one-eighth dog, Max, is a Chihuahua I inherited. He's fifteen years old, and will live to be about forty-nine, I'm thinking. The cat's named Nub, for obvious reasons. The real dogs—Sally, Lily, and Mabel—are some-where, we think, between four and eight years old. This is not a math quiz, I promise. I'm not going to make you think about a Trailways bus traveling thirty miles an hour from Point A in one direction, and a coyote traveling toward it from Point B at seventy miles an hour.

It's all about Mabel. Everything's about Mabel. Mabel wants it that way. Mabel considers nothing else. She must sleep with us. She must go wherever we go. If we watch a movie, she must spend time explaining how said movie's not as good as *My Dog Skip* or *Old Yeller*.

Mabel got thrown out by somebody, probably with her first litter, back in 2013. She circled our land in Dacusville, South Carolina, for three days, barking at me whenever I came out and tried to coax her my way. Her teats almost dragged the ground. I took out food. I took out water. Nub the cat had just shown up a couple of months earlier, and he looked at me as if to say, "Yeah, I remember that dog from the woods—she's a handful. She's needy. She's a trainload of neuroses."

Mabel's a brindle. She weighs thirty pounds, and Glenda got online and Googled "brindle, thirty pounds, big head, lolling tongue, yapping, untrustworthy" to find a photo of something that the American Kennel Club now recognizes as the Treeing Tennessee Brindle.

"I knew it!" Glenda said. "She's some kind of purebred dog that someone couldn't manage."

Here's an aside: When our beautiful dog Lily showed up in the front yard one morning at 5 a.m., she suffered from a variety of ailments. She was malnourished, she had cracked paw pads, and she didn't have toenails. She had canine scabies. Lily had been on the road for a while, obviously. When we got her stabilized, I took her to the vet, and beforehand Glenda, who'd been online and developed a theory, said, "Ask the vet what kind of dog she thinks Lily might be."

The vet plain said, "Mix of bird dog."

I came home and said, "You were right! Lily's a Welsh rabbit hound."

"I knew it!" Glenda blurted out. Then she hit me pretty hard in the arm when I told her the truth.

Anyway, back to Mabel. She circled. I went out in the woods looking for her litter, but found nothing. I assumed that coyotes, foxes, rabid raccoons, or some questionable people down the road happened upon the litter at some point earlier. I took food out—mix of kibble and the miracle cure for all sick dogs, Vienna sausages—

and crouched beneath a flowering crabapple. Mabel came close—like within ten yards—but hunched low, slunk, her eyes on me, and yipped.

"Maybe she doesn't like men," Glenda said.

And at that point Mabel—still unnamed by us—shot straight forward toward me. She didn't go for the food. I'm prone to exaggerate, I know, but I have a witness. This dog ran up to me as I still crouched and pressed the front of her belly up against me, her paws on my shoulders. She trembled something awful. I stroked her backbone. She finally released herself and devoured the still-bowled food at my feet.

Another aside: Armour Vienna Sausage, you can send royalty checks my way through EastOver Press.

At the time we still had a number of cast-off dogs: Dooley (RIP, died at age seventeen-plus), Nick, Maggie, Charlie, plus the aforementioned. All of this occurred about three months before Glenda and I moved to Spartanburg, South Carolina, from nearby Pickens County. I named Mabel; she seemed to come to that name in an inordinately quick time, as if maybe I'd guessed her original name, and I took her to the vet to get her some shots/get her spayed/have the vet check for a chip. Glenda said, "Hey ask the vet if she's a Treeing Tennessee brindle."

Mabel shook, quivered, and grunted—if there's a grunting Tennessee brindle, it's this dog—and I said, "What kind of dog is this?"

"Pit Bull mix," the veterinarian said.

I said, "Not a Treeing Tennessee brindle?"

The vet didn't smile. She looked me straight in the face. She said, "What?"

We moved to a couple acres of fenced-in yard. My old friends make fun of me. It's a compound. Come try to find me—it's impossible. There are twelve-foot-high tea olives surrounding the property, which hide the chain-link fence. There are thirteen magnolias. There's elaeagnus, which I just had to look up to see the correct spelling. That stuff smells good, especially while drinking good bourbon in its midst, whittling canes, reading Schopenhauer, staring at jet contrails overhead, thinking about the Bible, and/or wondering if there's any hope left in the world. There's false holly, and pines, and tulip poplars, and azaleas. Camellias, Japanese maples, a big spruce that doesn't belong here.

Still not a math test, I promise. All of this is to say, it's a damn perfect habitat for cardinals, wrens, chickadees, hummingbirds, goldfinches, bluebirds, one red-tailed hawk, chipmunks, anoles, opossums, skinks, rat snakes, one copperhead, one king snake, one rough green snake, and squirrels.

We have ten Yankee feeders scattered around, back yard and front yard. I fill them up about bi-daily with sunflower seeds. Oh to see male cardinals come down and hang out, or the doves down below. Some people think "bi-daily" means every other day. I mean "bi-freaking-daily."

Mabel might not be the smartest dog we've ever had. If we say, "Go for a ride?" or "You want a dog biscuit?" or "You want to go outside?" in that high-pitched voice that dog owners use, Sally, Lily, and one-eighth Max perk up. So does the cat. But not Mabel. She remains rolled over—I should mention, too, that she has eight nipples on one side of her belly, but only six on the other.

There's an emeritus professor named Dr. John Pilley who had a dog named Chaser who supposedly knew well over a thousand words. That dog has been on *60 Minutes,* among other shows. He was on a thing called *Cute Animals* starring Neil deGrasse Tyson, the astrophysicist.

We don't mention Chaser's name around Mabel, seeing as she's stuck on one word and one word only: Squirrel.

As I've already said, I can look Mabel in the eye and say, "You want a T-bone steak?" and she'll stare at me as if I've rattled off an algebra problem. But if I say, "Squirrel"—with zero inflection—she'll jump off the couch straight for the door, brindle tail out and straight, as if she derived from a regular AKC-recognized breed. She'll stare at the doorknob.

When I open the door, she takes off, paws in need of better traction, off the porch, down the pea gravel driveway, tiny pebbles ricocheting off our back car windows. Mabel skitters past the false holly, veering right, toward the first three-set of Yankee feeders where, indeed, squirrels hang upside down even though I've placed Slinkys down the posts as Glenda showed me to do after she saw something on the Facebook.

The squirrels ball up on themselves, fall to the ground, then hit the chain-link fence audibly, get through, or over, and hit sweet gum trees full tilt.

I stand on the deck, laugh, laugh-laugh-

laugh, and say, "Good dog, Mabel. You saved us! Good, good dog."

She looks up at the trees, turns to me, and — no hyperbole here — smiles. Smiling.

Treeing Tennessee dog. Smiling, odd-nippled, weirdo, attention-craving, grunting, lost-litter-mourning, smiling Treeing Tennessee brindle.

FIELD TRIPS FOR THE UNSUSPECTING

NO GOOD SMALL-TOWN South Carolina education can feel complete without a variety of educational, awe-inspiring field trips. When I went to college back in the mid-Seventies, I encountered students who matriculated from prep schools up north, and private schools in Florida and Atlanta. They talked about going to museums, plays, operas, and the like. One time in my first art history class, Dr. Sorenson showed a slide, and this nice red-haired kid raised his hand and said, "I think that slide's in backwards. We visited the Tate Museum my senior year in high school."

Jesus. The museum in Greenwood, which is still called "The Museum," housed a stuffed giraffe's neck and head, to be used as a banister when going upstairs to look at the old-timey blacksmith recreation, the old-timey apothecary, the old-timey cotton mill, maybe a couple of paintings done by a local artist depicting happy slaves in cotton fields. We had a rock collection, and arrowheads. There were other taxidermic displays: ducks, fox, raccoons, possums, every viper from the area, a swordfish. Not once in my art history class did I raise my hand in order to say, "I think that slide's in backwards, Dr. Sorenson. I went on a field trip to The Museum back in sixth grade, and I recall the beaver gazing off to the left, not the right."

I spent second and third grade at an elementary school called Merrywood, while the elementary school where I attended fourth through sixth grade got built within walking distance of my house. Within walking distance of Merrywood, luckily, was the wastewater treatment plant, where—in third grade—we got to stand on catwalks and look down at human feces swirling around while some guy in a hardhat told us that we could soon drink that water.

Also in third grade we boarded a passenger train in downtown Greenwood, before they tore up the tracks and dismantled the station, and rode it to Ninety-Six, some ten or twelve miles away. Then we stood around and rode another train back. I remember this particular field trip because a teacher named Mrs. Waymer—mean, and nothing like my teacher, Mrs. Shelley—yelled at me. I'd gotten up from my seat, gone to the head of the car, and jumped straight up. I thought that I—airborne—would end up in the very back. Of course I landed right back down from whence I jumped. (I don't understand physics. Also in college, when I couldn't take the right-wing Christians always trying to save me, I took off for France. This was back when one could smoke on a jet. I got drunk on the way between Atlanta and Gatwick, in London, walked up as far as I could before hitting the non-smoking section, jumped up in the aisle, and didn't land back by the miniature bathrooms.)

Aside: These two guys from Campus Crusade for Christ used to hang out nights in the laundry room in the basement of my freshman dorm. One of them said to me, "Have you accepted Jesus Christ as your Lord and Savior?" while I stood there waiting for my clothes to get through the rinse cycle. This was a time when I could pop my neck, left and right, and it sounded like a machine gun going off. I said, "The only way I'd believe in any of that mumbo-jumbo is if I broke my neck and lived to tell about it." Then I cracked my neck, fell on my knees, and yelled out, "It's a miracle." One guy laughed. The other guy said I would burn in Hell. I'm serious.

So there was The Museum, the shit factory, the train ride. And then, in twelfth grade, my psychology class and another one went on a field trip to Whitten Village, in Clinton, South Carolina, followed by the South Carolina State Hospital for the Insane, on Bull Street in Columbia. The state hospital had been called the South Carolina Lunatic Asylum for a long time, and most people just called it Bull Street.

My aunt Martha spent some time there, for what it's worth.

Whitten Village, only thirty miles from Greenwood, met the demands of sad, poor, birth-defected, mentally-challenged people, ranging from hydrocephalic to functional Down syndrome. I know these terms are no longer acceptable to use in polite society, but there were a number of waterheads and pinheads tragically dying in cribs there. Those were the "scientific" terms used in class back in 1975. We walked around as a group of forty students. We had our great psychology teacher with us—a smart, generous man named Mr. Blackman who wore a toupee that made Howard Cosell's look like real hair—plus my history teacher, an equally smart, kind of nervous woman named Mrs. Vincent who soon gave up teaching in order to sell real estate.

Of course, I kind of lagged behind. I got stuck talking to one of the residents, a tall Black man in his twenties, who had a series of short sutures spackled on his shaved head. I said, "What happened?"

He said, "I get the seizures." Whenever I watch the movie *Raising Arizona*, I think of this young man, for he spoke much like Hi's roommate in prison, the Black man brought up so poor that he ate dirt when there wasn't any crawfish left.

I don't remember anything else about the conversation. He seemed pretty normal to me—though I'll admit I had only half a semester's worth of high school psychology under my belt, nothing like an advanced degree.

I guess I caught up. I remember looking at this poor living being with a head the size of a pumpkin, the body of a standard Raggedy Ann.

We exited Whitten Village, and boarded our bus.

And then this: My suture-headed dude jumped out from behind a tree, his pants around his ankles, a smile spread across his face as if he'd just been tabbed the #1 Pick in the NBA lottery. He whacked off a pecker that had to be a foot long. I laughed, and pointed, and Mrs. Vincent yelled, "Drive! Drive! Drive!" even though not all of my classmates had taken seats.

I would imagine that we stopped for lunch. I don't remember packing a brown paper sack. But in my memory, we made it down I-26 to Columbia, exited on Elmwood Avenue, and took it to the front entrance to the insane asylum. We parked. We got out as a group.

Then, a patient up on the third floor of one of the buildings, grasping metal bars that covered the window, started yelling, "Fuck me! Fuck me! Fuck me!"

I don't remember Mr. Blackman's response. I know Mrs. Vincent wouldn't look up, and she shooed us inside. I looked for, but found no graffiti offered up by Aunt Martha.

I'm sorry, but I'd take this particular field trip over staring at a Constable or Gainsborough landscape of bleak men and women working the fields.

THE SEX SYMBOL
OF THE SOUTH

O H MAN OH MAN oh man oh man oh
man: Elmer Fudpucker, Sr. I have no
clue what any of this means, or how it
happened. Trust me on this one: A man named
Elmer Fudpucker, Sr., showed up at our house
more than once for three days at a time, back when
I might've been thirteen and fourteen years old.
He showed up in a black limousine, with a man
named Lester Vanadore. I didn't get it. Why
would these people be showing up to our little
1400 square foot house?

My father's friend Mr. Beasley, the public
defender, had something to do with it. Somehow, on the side, he worked Nashville singer/
songwriter contracts. I'm serious. And somehow, at least once, he brought Mr. Vanadore
and Elmer Fudpucker, Sr., down to Greenwood,
South Carolina.

Go to Google and type "Elmer Fudpucker,
Sr." See that photo from his album *Sex Symbol
of the South*. That dude. Famous among truckers
with eight-track players back in the day.

For some reason I thought that Lester
Vanadore worked as a manager for Elmer, but
that's not true. A.) Elmer's real name is Hollis

Champion; B.) Lester was a singer/songwriter in his own right.

Aside: While looking up shit I found out these two men had something to do with Mack Vickery, and that he wrote a song called "Meat Man," and that Jerry Lee Lewis covered it. It's amazing. Go listen to "Meat Man" and then come back here.

My mother died in December 2015, at the age of 87. I came across these albums of hers, one autographed to Bev, by Elmer Fudpucker. *The Sex Symbol of the South* got recorded at the Pulaski Lounge in Muskegon, Michigan. My mom was born and raised in Muskegon. Did she know more about Elmer than she ever acknowledged? Am I somehow related to Elmer...Fudpucker?

My parents held parties for these people that lasted three days. I hid in our basement. Upstairs, people came in and out. Music blasted the entire time. I'm not sure what happened to me over the years—I'll be the first person to wear a lamp-shade—but at the time I wanted nothing to do with a bunch of country-ass singers upstairs in my house drinking Smirnoff and eating my father's three-alarm Texas chili.

I hid. When I heard someone coming down the stairs, I escaped through a small door that led to the crawlspace of my parents' house. I slunk around, I pouted, I made myself invisible. The music poured in from upstairs, and the Sex Symbol of the South's voice—high and twangy as cat gut pulled to its limits, then plucked with a sharp-ended finger—raged on.

Years later, and daily, I underwent this same feeling while I wrote. I hid alone. Voices merged and rebounded and clanked against each other.

My friends came over and my mother sent them down to the basement to find me. Their parents sent them over. Their parents thought someone — probably my father — died. Why else would a funeral home's limousine be parked in our driveway?

Aside: My first trip to Nashville took place in the mid-1980s. I'm not the biggest country music fan, but I am a fan of seedy bars. On Lower Broad, I walked into a place called The Music City Lounge, across from Tootsie's Orchid. The Music City Lounge, of course by now, has been replaced with a Hard Rock Cafe, or Gap, or Planet Fitness. Anyway, I walked in and looked at the band to find, of course, Elmer Fudpucker in front of the microphone, singing songs about trucking, truck drivers, the secret of lovemaking, et cetera. What are the chances? I thought.

During the band's break I walked up — he'd not seen me in over a decade — and re-introduced myself. I explained my parents, my hometown, his lawyer Mr. Beasley, the limo. I understand that someone of Elmer Fudpucker, Sr.'s fame might cause him to forget people and places, or incidents, but the way he stared at me, mouth open, hair oddly-coiffed, made me wonder if I'd dreamed up the entire past scenarios.

BACK FROM THE GRAVE

OOD-TO-BE STRAYS thrown out in the middle of the country by impatient and/or unready dog owners invariably crawl on their bellies, eyes up and pleading. I've never lived with loving and judicious ex-strays that didn't appear in my yard, then come to me as if mimicking a Parris Island soldier-in-training forced to crawl beneath razor wire. River showed up thusly, as did Gypsy, Lily, and Sally. All my other ex-strays over the years—Nick, Maggie, Stella, Marty, et al—have been great dogs in their own ways, but they've never fully shaken the feral out of their coats.

My dog Dooley appeared on March 1, 2000. I went out to the front yard at dawn with my then nine-year-old dog River. Fog hung low. I could see my neighbor's mother-in-law a hundred yards away, a new dog beside her. I yelled out, "Hey, Dot, did Jim get a new dog?"

With this, Dooley came running toward River and me. River—one of those mixed breeds that look like coyotes—didn't growl, bark, or wag her tail. Dot yelled back, "No. That's not our dog."

Dooley—white and liver spotted, mostly legs, thin as a whisper—dropped onto his belly, eyes up, with what looked like a smile. He crawled past a Leyland cypress, a fig tree that appeared to be a bonsai, and a crabapple tree. He reached River. They touched noses. I won't lie here: At the time, Glenda and I had eight ex-stray dogs and Herb the ex-stray cat controlling us, all of which emerged from the tree farm across the road, and I thought, I need to take this boy down to the Humane Society.

Dooley followed River and me inside. I put a bowl of dry food down for him and said to Glenda, "See if anyone wants a dog over at the school," et cetera. On this particular day I had to drive to a detention center for juvenile delinquents in Alabama to teach fiction writing, oddly. I needed to get on the road, and wouldn't return for three days. "We can't afford another dog," I said. I meant it, too.

I came home from my little trip. Dooley sat in the laundry room, chewing on the molding. "No one wants a dog," Glenda said. "He's a great dog. He's tried to eat through the wall and the half-door, but he's house-trained."

To this day—twelve years later—I have no clue how hard Glenda tried to find the dog another home.

Here's Dooley between March 2000 and Labor Day Weekend 2010: Whenever I pick up car keys, he runs to the door. When there's a bird, squirrel, or rabbit some-where outside, he's staring out the window. If I yell, "cow," "horse," or "Republican," he'll run to the window and bark. When I go off on book tours, Glenda says, he won't eat, and barely leaves my writing room. He lived with me at Wrightsville Beach for five weeks and stared at seabirds nonstop. He's curled up below me as I write this. River died at the age of fourteen, and since then Dooley's been the official greeter and tester-outer of two more strays who showed up. He's our largest dog, but the gentlest. He's that dog.

A week before Labor Day in 2010, I had to put our dog Marty — nineteen years old — down. I buried him next to Ann, Hershey, River, Inklet, Nutmeg, Joan, and a stray we'd been trying to coax over for a month that some overzealous DNR agent shot in the tree farm. Nineteen! One time when I wasn't paying attention, Marty — part bulldog, mostly underbite — had stuck his head in my plastic cup and drank about sixteen ounces of a bourbon and Coke. He wobbled around, peed on himself, and then wouldn't come near booze for the rest of his life. I buried him deep, and placed some chicken wire and a cement block on the grave.

Seven days later I ventured way in the back yard to ride a stationary bike I keep out of sight so that I don't ride it too often, and I said, "What smells? Something's dead out here."

I got off the bike and found — oh, no — Marty's back leg pushed out of his grave. It seems as though Lily and Sally — two feisty ex-strays — had tunneled in from the side. I shaded my eyes, for some reason, and pushed Marty back in. I dug a hole and threw that hard clay back over the grave, tamped it down, put the chicken wire back down, placed some tin roofing over about a four-by-eight foot area, found some hurricane fencing to cover the tin, and then covered the area with eight cement blocks. There are smaller grave sites for world leaders than the one Marty now has.

That night, at about ten o'clock, Dooley threw up a bowl of undigested food. I said, "Damn, Dooley, what's wrong?" I cleaned up the mess.

He drank a half bowl of water and vomited.

I cleaned that up and took him into Glenda's studio instead of my writing room.

He drank water, he couldn't keep it down—this went on until dawn. Even though I had done well in a college logic course, I didn't make a connection between some things. I thought that Dooley had an obstruction—one time years earlier our dog Ann ingested a number of unripe peaches that fell off the tree, skinnied up, and the veterinarian ended up giving her a simple enema that cost us $250 to get thirty peach pits out of her system.

I took Dooley outside and gave him the same treatment—I'll jump ahead and say that he wouldn't look me in the face for a few good days after this—but to no avail.

I drove him into Greenville to the emergency vet clinic. This was a Sunday. Evidently it was Hit a Dog in Greenville Day, too, for Dooley and I sat there for a good three hours before a vet could see him. At this point—he didn't seem dehydrated yet, he wasn't throwing up—he seemed fine.

I took him home, he drank water and released it accordingly.

Twenty-four hours later, he could barely stand. I picked him up and got him back to the emergency clinic, where a great veterinarian named Dr. B.J. Rogers—whom I'd dealt with in the past when Stella needed an emergency hysterectomy—said, "He's too dehydrated to do exploratory surgery. The X-ray shows nothing, but I know there's something in there. We can do a sonogram later."

That look on her face let me know he might not make it. She left the room. Glenda touched my shoulder. I cried, cried, cried.

When Dr. Rogers came back in, I said, "Whatever it takes," but my voice came out all squeaky.

She said, "Go on home. We'll try to get him strong enough."

Back home, I walked back to the graveyard to make sure the dogs hadn't befouled my Marty grave. On the way I kept finding torn pieces of towel—the towel we'd wrapped Marty in before burying him.

I called up Dr. Rogers and said, "You're going to find pieces of towel in his intestines. He evidently ate a towel." I didn't go into detail. I wouldn't want the veterinarian thinking that we were some kind of low rent, towel-wrapping, dog-burying people in Dacusville.

She said, "Yep. We found it on the sonogram."

Dooley survived the surgery, barely. He stayed at the clinic for a couple days, but they didn't want to release him because he'd not peed. I showed up—he looked terrible—and said, "Let me just take him home." When I got him outside on a leash, he peed for ten minutes on the grass—it seemed as though he knew not to pee inside, on a concrete floor. In my mind Dooley can do no wrong, outside of saying to Lily and Sally, "Hey give me that towel. If y'all eat it, you might get sick." What a martyr!

My friend Ron Rash called me up a couple weeks after this incident. He said, "What's been going on?" I started to tell him the entire story. When I got to "towel," he said, "Are you making fun of me?"

"What?"

And then he told me about how his own dog, Ahab, had pulled a pair of Ron's boxer shorts out of the dirty clothes, eaten them, and then undergone the same surgery as Dooley, by the same veterinarian. *What's going on with these dogs who live with writers?* I wondered. *Is there something to reincarnation? Were they critics in a previous life?* I like to think that's the case— that Dooley once roamed this earth as a critic or editor, and that he's at my feet now sending me high-frequency advice only I can discern. "Write about me, write about me, write about me," he's probably communicating now. "Tell everyone about my fearless exploits."

CHAINS

OUTSIDE OF THE walking-out-of-church episode back when I was seven years old, the other seminal event during my childhood, I imagine, occurred during the first week of my seventh grade year—August, 1970, the first year of integration. Up until this point my hometown held the white schools Merrywood, Matthews, Pinecrest, and Leslie Elementary schools, among others, perhaps. There was (White) Northside and (White) Southside junior highs, and (White) Greenwood High school—home of the Emeralds. Emeralds! Like there was some kind of gemstone mine nearby.

There was Brewer Elementary, Brewer Junior High, and Brewer High School for the Black populace. Surely there was more than one Black elementary school prior to 1970—the town had to have been split 50/50 Black and White—but I don't recall any. Hell, the Black hospital was Brewer Hospital.

So integration happened. Good. Finally I could go sit up in the balcony of the old State movie theatre—which later became The Little Theatre, next to The Museum. For years I'd wanted to climb those outside fire escape metal steps and see a movie from above, but couldn't because of my skin color.

We integrated, and nothing but fights and violence ensued. There were riots. It made the national news. This was a time before every seventh grader in America had access to pistols, but a bunch of them showed up—Black and White—with chains.

School got cancelled for two weeks. Some changes had to take place, some parameters set in place. No school for a solid ten days.

Except for those students voted on to the Bi-racial Committee.

Listen, I'd been around Black kids and adults the entire time I lived in Greenwood, all of five years. My grandfather had a man named Eddie Cannon who worked with him—there'd been a fire at my grandfather's business, and Eddie Cannon got burned up coming back in to save my grandfather. Later on, my father hired out Mr. Cannon to do various jobs. My father had a friend named Mr. Ebo who lived in a shingle-sided house out on Deadfall Road, and we visited at times. Mr. Ebo had a niece (I think, at least some kind of relative) named Shirley, who attended Pinecrest Elementary pre-integration—a young, tall, beautiful girl I've written about in *The Half-Mammals of Dixie* and *Why Dogs Chase Cars.* Deadfall Road wasn't but a mile from Pinecrest, so I assume that's why she went there.

I remained on the Bi-racial Committee for three years, then even in high school.

I just found my seventh-grade yearbook and looked to see if there was a photograph of the Bi-racial Committee. There's not. There are photos of some of the richer kids, playing basketball, or cheerleading, but nothing about the Bi-racial Committee. I don't remember the other White kids in this little club, but Jackie Sanders and Cheryl Puckett were on it. We sat in a room for two weeks. They stroked my hair and said, "You have the softest hair ever." I became fascinated with their palms, and the white soles of their feet. I fell in love.

I cannot remember one thing we did during those two weeks. We hung out in a classroom. We talked about nothing. I bet we had to play role-playing games, which I detest on the level of charades, of course. We shrugged at one another. I'm sure some kind of seventh-grade philosophical views got aired on par with Rodney King's "Can't we all just get along?" I remember only white palms and white soles, hair-stroking.

Well, I remember someone saying to me, "Stick it in easy, and it come back greasy," but I wasn't quite sure what she meant.

NU-WAY LOUNGE
AND RESTAURANT

EVERYONE'S HEARD ABOUT the Nu-Way Lounge and Restaurant's Redneck Cheeseburger served with a secret-recipe pimento cheese atop the patty — it's won awards, and been featured both in national print media and on television. Regulars know about the White Trash Burger with jalapeños, and the Trailer Park Burger on buttered toast. There's the Blu-Way chicken sandwich, and the Nu-Wayler fish sandwich. There's PBR, Miller, Bud, and then — for the more adventurous — Corona, Guinness, and Red Stripe. The wine list goes like this: "red, white, or pink." It's pretty well known that Nu-Way celebrated its seventy-fifth anniversary last year, at its original spot at 373 East Kennedy Street in downtown Spartanburg, South Carolina. There's the red front door, a bar with a handful of tables running its length, a "dining room" to the side, and an outdoor patio behind the place protected by a wooden fence. There are a couple of old-fashioned pinball machines, and one of those bowling games.

So I don't need to write about all that.

I had frequented Nu-Way six or eight times

over a twenty year period, back when I lived in Dacusville, South Carolina, some fifty miles away. At times I needed to come to Spartanburg for book signings or readings, and I said, "Hey, can we go to Nu-Way, can we go to Nu-Way, can we go to Nu-Way?" which, perhaps, irritated my hosts in ways that New Yorkers understand when visitors plead to visit the Statue of Liberty or Charlestonians when it comes to Market Street and the Hunley submarine.

Sometimes my hosts indulged me, but these were usually English department-type people, so there was no casual conversations at the bar. Instead, the table-talk concerned lesser-known short stories of William Faulkner, the postmodern musings of Jacques Derrida, tales of what someone said or did at the last writers' conference. Other times someone in the group would blurt out, "I need a salad!" or "It's too smoky in here!" or—even after Spartanburg banned smoking in restaurants and bars—"I can still smell smoke in there!"

An aside: There are five salad options on the menu, from Classic House to Cobb. In between is the Classic Cheeseburger Salad.

Aside #2: People who "can still smell smoke in there" usually drive cars that emit toxic gases, and they need to move into a hole in the ground, or to Antarctica.

So. Last year I accepted a position in the English department at one of the local colleges, in Spartanburg. My better half, Glenda, and I bought a house in mid-March. I immediately started painting what would become my office—that's another story that involves a jungle mural on the walls with giraffes, rhinos, lion, tigers, gorillas, Jesus, lemurs, a dachshund, fish, flora. Noah's crashed ark on Mount Ararat, elephants, and an eagle on the ceiling—and began moving books and books and books. My dog Dooley helped out as best as he could, on weekends and late workday afternoons.

I said to Dooley one mid-afternoon Saturday, "Hey, let's go to Nu-Way."

We went. I parked, and put the windows two-thirds down for him, and went inside. I said to Becky, the owner who worked the grill on this particular day, "I want a Redneck Burger, and I need a plain burger with nothing on it for my dog."

She said, "Your dog's outside?" I nodded. She said, "You got a leash? You can bring him in."

I said, "Yeah, I do. How nice," and got Dooley out of the Jeep.

I don't want to get all existential and dog-whispering about this, but when I brought Dooley in I pretty much felt him saying, "Wow! Thanks! Can we play that bowling game?"

Becky said, "I got a couple hot dogs, too, I'll give him free." Dooley sat down on the floor, on his best behavior. Soon thereafter he ate from my hand as thirteen-year-old dogs are wont to do. Again, not to get all anthropomorphic, but I could tell my dog wanted to say, "This is what everyone should be talking about when they mention Nu-Way."

A half week went by. I needed help moving a 6,000 pound bookcase. I got this buddy of mine to drive over because he owed me. We'd moved an 8,000 pound bookcase of his the previous summer on a 105-degree day. My buddy had gone to seminary at Duke, which figures into this story. I said, "Hey, Mark, even though you didn't offer me a sip of water last summer, let me take you to this place called the Nu-Way, on me," et cetera.

He said, "Can I smoke a cigar in there?"

I said, "Sure," lying, because I didn't go to seminary.

I'll admit that some of the story so far has been filled with hyperbole, but this part's not: The man behind the grill, Andrew, had just graduated from Duke seminary. He was a friend of Becky's family, and she needed help behind the grill. Andrew had come back home to work as a chaplain at one of the hospitals. I learned this information because I'll talk to ants inhabiting the crack of a sidewalk, and I sat down saying to anyone who might listen, "Hey. I came in here Saturday with my dog. Becky fed him some free food. What's your story?" and so on.

The man to the left of me said, "My daddy was a Hall of Fame basketball coach over at Erskine College," and I said, ""Coach Red Myers?" And he said, "Yeah," and I said, "I met your sister one time at a bar in Hodges called Jackson Station."

Red Myers's son was a pharmacist who went by Dubb. A man on the other side of Mark said, "I went to Wofford. This bar used to be different before they changed the drinking age from eighteen to twenty-one, back in 1986 or so."

Mark asked Andrew if Dr. So-and-So still taught at the seminary, and they might've started talking about Faulkner, Derrida, and various conferences involving Methodists. I looked around. A man named Andrew Blanchard said, "Welcome to Spartanburg, George," from behind me at a table. We'd met in Oxford, Mississippi, nine years earlier, before he took a job in the art department at Converse College. A group of men and women sporting nice tattoos showed up soon thereafter. A lawyer came in talking about how he didn't want another day like this one. Up by the door sat two White and two Black men, laughing, pointing up at the TV. Somebody played the jukebox. Johnny Cash came on, followed by the Pogues.

No one sat mesmerized by a smartphone.

It's that place. Nu-Way's more about being a melting pot than it is a place for a patty melt.

Every idiot running for elected office has visited. But here's what I like to think: During World War II some 200,000 enlistees entered Camp Croft—just four miles from Nu-Way—between 1941 and 1945. Remember, Nu-Way opened in 1938. Soldiers received weekend passes during their training exercises. Some of the more famous Camp Croft residents included actor Zero Mostel, Nixon's buddy Henry Kissinger, Edward Koch, sports broadcaster Mel Allen, Nixon's other buddy Spiro Agnew, Thomas Wolfe's brother Fred, and the great short story writer John Cheever.

You know one or more of them sat at the same bar top. Can you imagine the conversation between Agnew, Koch, and Mostel, Mel Allen giving a play-by-play? Or Kissinger saying, "Let me try this pimento cheese everyone keeps talking about"?

Man. I love wondering if John Cheever sat inside this bar at some point, looking straight ahead, thinking, *This place gives me ideas.*

MOON PIE

F I HEARD SOMEONE talking about Moon
Pie between the late 1970s and early '80s in
upstate South Carolina, I knew it wasn't a
reference to the wondrous confection hailing
from Chattanooga. Nope, they would have been
talking about the best goddamn rock and roll
band ever invented that hadn't yet made it to
the big time. I came to know this quartet from
my college buddy Michael Hunt—now a theatre
professor in Virginia—a man one year older than
me in age and about forty years older in music
and literature experience. "Come with me to see
the best goddamn rock band ever that hasn't yet
made it—Moon Pie," he said. He knew these
guys, who were a few years older, because they
all went to the same high school in Greenville.
"I want to take you by the church to see them,"
he said.

Of course, I thought, *What?* Had Michael
converted to Protestantism without my
knowing? I said, "Moon Pie. Really?" It
sounded overly southern to me. I imagined
bands named RC Cola, Red Man Chewing
Tobacco, Collard Greens. This was 1979. Already
I'd jumped from the Grateful Dead to the Sex
Pistols, the Clash, the Ramones, et al. And I'd
somehow never cottoned to the stereotypical

southern rock bands of my time—though I loved the Allman Brothers, and admired Marshall Tucker. And this Moon Pie band was from South Carolina! How good could they be, really? "What kind of music do they play?" I asked.

"Just shut the fuck up and come on," Michael said. "They don't sound like anybody."

The lineup changed over the years, but the band I met and knew was Doug Whelchel on drums, Tommy Tate on bass, Lynn "Roy Moon" Rochester on lead guitar, and Gerald Duncan as the rhythm guitarist and lead singer. Dick Hodgin—who had one working eye, a source of self-deprecating jokes—was the band's sound man and manager, and he later produced a five-song EP by an unknown group named Hootie and the Blowfish. Dick might've been Rob Reiner's influence to have the volume turned up to eleven in *This is Spinal Tap*.

Gerald, clearly, fronted the band. He wrote most of the songs. His stage presence made John Malkovich and Richard Burton look like amateurs. As for the other members—and no offense to my friends—their stage presence didn't look much different than a small-town police lineup.

The "church" was "The Church of Rock 'n' Roll," as early local journalists labeled it, in downtown Greenville, on Townes Street. I never knew what happened to the original church and its flock, but whoever owned the building allowed these ne'er-do-wells to rent space for practice.

Michael and I walked in. He introduced me around, maybe told everyone I was okay, not a narc. Understand that in 1979 I had decided I might want to be a writer of sorts. I'd just returned from studying in France. Boy, did I know everything! Wouldn't it be both charming and gracious for me to impart my wisdom, at age twenty-one, to these fellers in a band named after a lunch-box treat? My god, these guys hadn't even gone to college, unless you counted Gerald's matriculation from Eastside High School — where he was student body president — to the Hank Thompson School of Country Music in Claremore, Oklahoma.

The Church of Rock 'n' Roll attracted a bizarre mix of people, I thought at the time, groupies milling around right before Moon Pie went to the stage to work on songs they'd written the previous week, maybe "Two Girls in Love" or "Down to the Graveyard." Maybe "Jenny," about a young woman who "is a switchblade," or "Regina," which concerned an interracial relationship. The Moon Pie fanatics, as it turned out — people I thought were wannabe artists, writers, actors, comedians, musicians, professors, lawyers — actually thrived later (all of them, I can count them off) as artists, writers, actors, and so on.

The band started up. Within about thirty minutes I understood that Moon Pie, indeed, couldn't be categorized. Nowadays, I can say they might've been at the forefront of Americana, or cowpunk. They came across as a mix of Willie Nelson and Elvis Costello, of Buddy Rich and Graham Parker.

In clubs and bars they played ninety-minute shows, at the least, filled with three- to four-minute narratives about living in a town and wanting to get out, being away from home and wanting to return, hating a job, being unemployed and willing to work for the worst boss ever. Unrequited love. Main Street drag racing. Bad, bad radio station formats. Moon Pie was a mix of Springsteen, the Modern Lovers, Hank Williams, and the Blasters. Some years later I saw Jason and the Scorchers—a band I love—and thought, *Moon Pie, back in the day.*

Moon Pie dropped one EP, *Welcome to Hard Times*, but Gerald became disenchanted with Greenville's live music opportunities and moved to Raleigh. The band changed its name to The Accelerators and signed with Dolphin Records, and then Profile, and toured the United States, playing New York City to Los Angeles, opening for the Clash and Nick Lowe. At some point, Rochester and Tate decided not to stay in the band. The lead guitar lineup changed a couple of times, as did the bass player. Eventually, Brad Rice—later with Son Volt and then Keith Urban—became the lead guitarist. Gerald remained the heartbeat and backbone, and despite the promising reviews of its albums, the label, after releasing Run-DMC's first album, made a decision to fully embrace rap artists and take a new direction.

And that's how a Greenville band that once called itself Moon Pie could've been, could've been, could've been.

MARKING TERRITORY

THE CAT DIDN'T get hurt physically. I don't know how to measure a cat's psychological damage due to insult and embarrassment, but if there's any chance a mean old house cat can comprehend outright embarrassment, then this particular Darlington cat suffered enough to make a pet psychologist wealthy, I'm sure. I'm not saddened. I do stay awake still—these twenty years later—in fear that this old tom will show up outside my door, but that might have to do with other paranoid tendencies on my part.

I will change the names. I can't even remember the stupid cat's name, so I'll go with Zorro—and I will come out of this, I'm sure, as an idiot. An idiot and a heel. So I'm going to plead my case from near the beginning of the end.

I'll call her Ms. Pearson, because David Pearson was a great stock-car legend, and this particular ex-girlfriend shared the name of another stock-car legend. Not Petty or Waltrip or Earnhardt. Not Fireball Roberts. Another one. This all took place in Darlington, South Carolina, home to a racetrack known to be "Too Tough to Tame." I was twenty-nine, then thirty, and she was about twenty-five. Ms. Pearson looked a lot like that Cybil Shepherd actress. Not that I'm a bastion of responsibility or rational behavior, but sometimes she acted like the woman in *Sybil*, the movie.

It all came down to Ms. Pearson's frequent AA meetings—she didn't drink, and from what I remember she never had partaken of the drink, but she believed in that genetic theory of alcoholism—and my disdain for AA meetings. Maybe I was wrong, looking back on it.

Also, I need to throw another cog into this dysfunctional relationship. I'll call him the Remora. I worked with the Remora—a remora's better known as a suckerfish to anyone who is not an ichthyologist—and his girlfriend had left him. I can't use her name either, but I swear to god it wasn't that far from being Fifi or any other poodle-like name. Fifi left the Remora, and then he kept calling me up to say, "Hey, I'm really lonely, man. If you and Ms. Pearson go out this weekend, keep me in mind," et cetera.

So I'd call. I didn't want a suicide on my conscience. That has to count for something. I couldn't stand thinking about a poor guy sitting alone in his house, pining for Fifi, a giant bottle of Bufferin on his lap, which he'd use as a call for help.

I should mention at this point that Ms. Pearson and I lived in the same house—owned by her grandmother—but I had to park a few blocks away each night so her grandmother wouldn't drive by in the morning and see my truck. She was a matriarch straight off a bad soap opera. Anyway, Ms. Pearson and I lived in the same house, split the rent money she paid her grandmother, and there was also that mean cat Zorro that Ms. Pearson loved. This cat—on the very first date with Ms. Pearson—came out of another room and attacked my ankle. He shredded my sock and scratched me so deeply I bled. He never blinked over the entire six months or year or however long the relationship lasted. Ms. Pearson kept a Dixie cup on top of the litter box, so that when the cat used it she would immediately scoop out his business and flush it down the toilet. The cat waited for me around corners daily, and the girlfriend sat around within eyeshot of the litter box's front door at all times.

The litter box comes back into play in this story.

The Remora would go out with us, usually to a bar on the Darlington square. He'd be all hangdog-faced. He kept a pocketful of quarters and paid for his draft beer thusly, as if the bar was only a side trip on his way to the laundromat. When Ms. Pearson would excuse herself to go pee out six gallons of Coke and water and iced tea, the Remora would always say, "Man, I don't know how you can take it. She sure does bitch a lot about your drinking. That's got to be rough. How can you take it? She sure does bitch a lot about your drinking," on and on.

Then, from what I learned later, when I went to rid myself of, say, a dozen beers and dozen shots of bourbon, the Remora would say to Ms. Pearson, "Man, I don't know how you can take it. George sure drinks a lot. That's got to be rough. How can you take it? He sure does drink a lot."

Classic Remora M.O., I later learned from either the Learning Channel, the Discovery

Channel, or a *Wikipedia* entry I may or may not have written myself later on in life.

For some reason, I moved out of the house, but she and I kept dating. Maybe her grandmother discovered the arrangement, I don't know. Maybe the cat sent me some kind of subtle, subliminal messages while I slept. More than likely—looking back—Ms. Pearson tired of my coming home late and passing out, and she rightly figured I'd never amount to much more than an idiot itinerant English instructor working semester to semester on an adjunct basis, trying to teach future plumbers and welders the importance of complete sentences. Or maybe my eye strayed toward women without a love for sock-shredding felines. In my defense, I didn't know I suffered from "stray eye." I didn't even know it was an official syndrome until I saw it on *Oprah*. Or read about it on *Wikipedia*.

Anyway, I moved into a four-room house about three hundred yards away. Ms. Pearson moved some of her belongings, or at least a highboy, into my little brick place. I kept a desk and typewriter at hers, for some reason. More often than not, I kept my truck parked at my house and scurried over to hers after dark. The one time I drove over there and parked, she woke up the next morning, got in her own car, and rammed into my passenger-side door. Ms. Pearson always promised she didn't mean to do it. She did so with a slight smile on her face, kind of like when Cybil Shepherd smirked at Bruce Willis in that old *Moonlighting* show.

We split up, we made up. The Remora continued his long, arduous, timed plan of attack until, finally, Ms. Pearson said that she and I could no longer see each other. I guess she finally realized I wasn't going to change anytime soon, that it was hopeless to wait around to see if I'd ever get published, quit drinking, and be kinder to the ones closest to me as opposed to complete strangers. I do not think she made a bad decision there.

Maybe a week passed before Ms. Pearson came over to my house to get that stupid highboy thing back. I'm not even sure why it ever seemed necessary to have this giant piece of furniture taking up so much of my so-called den. It's not like I owned an array of raincoats and slickers and ponchos to hang on the thing. I didn't have extra blankets to put in the bottom part of it. She came over to get it, and she said, "I have a date on Friday night."

Perhaps I said, "Good for you," but I doubt it. I said, "You know, this highboy is probably going to topple over on the way to your house. You're going to have to sit on it to weigh it down."

Like I said, it was only a few blocks away, but involved a sharp descent and two or three hairpin turns. Ms. Pearson said, "Don't do anything stupid," and climbed into the bed of my pickup.

I said, "I'll be careful."

Then I took a left-hand turn instead of going straight across Mechanicsville Road. Ms. Pearson sat on the highboy, looking, I imagined, like the queen of England. Or maybe the queen of whatever country had a good-looking empress.

I drove straight onto the Darlington square, and—I'm not sure how I got all the lights to work in my favor—drove laps, my right hand on the horn, my left holding the steering wheel as hard as any stock-car driver trying to maneuver a track Too Tough to Tame. People looked at Ms. Pearson riding in back. In my mind, I saw her staring straight ahead—or behind—not waving the classic queen salute, but clenching her strong jaw in a way that only correct women can clench.

So on that Friday—I hate to admit it, but I'd gotten kind of depressed over this woman understanding I would not change my self-destructive ways—I left my job teaching college English and drove straight over to The Remora's house. I thought, *I was there for him during all those crybaby sessions, so he owes me.* The Remora lived near a blue-collar bar I liked called Rosie's.

Aside: One time I was in Rosie's and this man with a jet-black, hard pompadour said, "My name's spelled D-A-U-G-H-N. I'm one of only about four people in the world who has the name Don spelled that way." I was with a good Irish ex-All-American distance runner named Jim Haughey, who said to Daughn, "I know about three thousand men named Daughn back home, spelled that way."

Daughn pulled out a pistol and aimed it at Jim. I said something like, "Whoa, whoa, whoa," and tried to push the barrel back toward the bar. Daughn said to Jim, "I think you're some kind of spy. Who're you working for?" and so on.

Daughn, from what I understood later, got sent to prison soon thereafter for other reasons.

Anyway, I drove my banged-in truck to The Remora's house to find, of course, Ms. Pearson's car parked in his driveway. Only later — the next morning — would I find out she was going out on a date with him, that he would drive her all the way down to Murrells Inlet sixty miles away, and that he would say she was the prettiest woman in the seafood restaurant. If The Remora ordered shark off the menu, would that make him even more of a traitor? Answer: Yes.

So I went to Rosie's alone and drank a few beers. Then I drove to the next bar on my way home and drank a few beers. There are a lot of roadhouse bars in the swampy Pee Dee region of South Carolina, by the way. I went to the next place, then the next, finally ending up at the bar on the square I frequented more often than not, a place called Zorka's.

I told my tale of woe to the bartender, who was also named George, and to anyone else who'd listen. I made people make vows to curse The Remora whenever they ran into him again. And then I realized it was absolutely necessary I drive my truck over to Ms. Pearson's house, hop over the back fence, jimmy open the unlocked back window, and retrieve my desk and an arm lamp and the extra typewriter I still had over there.

I did so. Then I got to thinking about how, maybe, The Remora and Ms. Pearson might end up at the house later, so I found a photo album, pulled out all the photographs she had of me, and taped them on the den wall.

I could've unlocked the front door, packed up my truck, returned inside to make sure the back window was shoved down, and so on. I could've made it out of there.

But I looked at the cat. He sat hunched near his litter box, staring at me. He waited for me to look away, or busy myself with something else, so he could pounce.

I said, "You stupid son of a bitch," and walked toward him. He scrammed into the bedroom.

The litter box was a fancy one with a hood that attached with four side clamps. I unclamped the things and lifted the lid. All those beers, certainly, had built up.

I might've peed two gallons into the litter box. I'm talking the cat litter floated up. I secured the lid, told the cat to have a nice life with The Remora, and left.

Understand, I didn't bang into any of her possessions. I didn't torch the place or go over to The Remora's and crash into whichever car was left in the driveway there. I didn't shoot out any lights, harm an animal, short out the electrical circuit. I just peed in her litter box. Then I drove home and thanked god for the Darlington cops' absence in my life on this particular evening.

I awoke to someone knocking repeatedly on my door at six in the morning. I heard Ms. Pearson yelling out my name. I got off the bed and thought, uh-oh—she's going to be pissed off about all those pictures I taped on the wall. What if the Scotch tape takes off some paint, and then her grandmother asks what happened?

I opened the door to find Ms. Pearson standing there, crying. Her car was parked beside my truck, in the yard. She left it running. She blubbered. I said, "Hey. What? What's the matter with you?"

I couldn't make this up, and it's exactly how I've told the story for the past two decades. Ms. Pearson blurted out, "I need you to help me get the cat to a veterinarian. I think his bladder burst!"

At that moment, to be honest, I'd forgotten all about peeing in the litter box. I remembered breaking into the house and getting my stuff, and about the photos, but not invading the cat's personal space. I said, "Hey, I saw your car over at — — —-'s house"—this was before I called him The Remora—"yesterday. What're you doing going out with him, anyway? Is that the kind of weasel you're looking for?" I might've gone on and on.

She said, "He went into his litter box, and then he came out shaking his front and back paws like crazy. I looked in there and it's filled up." She spoke about the cat, not The Remora.

Then I recalled everything from eight or nine hours earlier. I started laughing and said, "His bladder didn't burst, fool. I peed in his cat box last night."

She quit crying. I'm talking she turned off the tears just a little too fast. I think Ms. Pearson knew all along. Composed, she evidently decided this would be the perfect time to let me in on all that stuff about going out on a date to Murrells Inlet, being called the prettiest girl in the restaurant, and so on.

But I could tell she wasn't ecstatic about The

Remora. I don't want to brag or claim sooth-saying capabilities or anything, but I think that, deep down, she wanted a man in her life who did things like pee in the cat box. I think she wanted a little danger and excitement and unpredictability in her life, though she wouldn't admit it on a Saturday morning, her cat in one of those pet traveler things that don't look a whole lot different from fancy-lidded litter boxes.

She called me an asshole and left. Her relationship with the Remora lasted about another two dates, from what I understand. He stayed away from me, then went off to finish his Ph.D. and write a dissertation called something like "Passive-Aggressive Tendencies in the Works of F. Scott Fitzgerald" or "T.S. Eliot Really Needed Ezra Pound" or "Truman Capote's Workout Regimen" or "I Rode on Peter Benchley's Underbelly While He Wrote *Jaws*."

My next real relationship was with a woman who owned a pit bull.

Ms. Pearson ended up marrying a man who played drums for a band that did cover songs in hotel lounges. They moved to Kentucky. The cat, I'm sure, acclimated well there. I turned out okay and even have a cat, along with all these ex-stray dogs. I don't play tricks on my cat. The dogs do.

WHY I FEAR GUNS, BUTCHER BLOCKS, AND NON-UNIONIZED MANUAL LABOR

I COULDN'T COUNT the number of times my father said to me, "Come work for me today. I'll pay you five dollars an hour." Five dollars an hour! That was something like three dollars and thirty-five cents above minimum wage!

These promises occurred on Saturdays and Sundays mostly. I would go out and run early, get back, take a shower, then go off with my father to his little business in Hodges, South Carolina.

More often than not, here's what happened: the splitting machine, which had a thirteen-foot band blade that ran clockwise behind some questionable finger guards, would be running perfectly. Any sane person would say, "Man, that old splitting machine, built in the 1940s, is something else."

But my father was never satisfied. He'd struggle down on his hands and knees and start taking the thing apart. He'd hand me grease-covered bolts and say, "Don't never say I never gave you nothing. Quadruple negative!" because I, smart-assed, forever corrected his grammar, especially double-negatives.

We'd ease open the guards, take the blade out using needle-nosed pliers, and take out the feed roll, setting all of these parts down on a compromised linoleum floor. This might have taken anywhere from thirty minutes to an hour. Then he'd say, "Let's go shoot the gun."

My father wasn't some kind of weapons expert or collector. He never hunted. For some reason he owned a thirty-ought-six, and a long-barreled .22 pistol.

Aside: When I was twelve, my father took me out the back door of our brick house, onto the square red brick patio. He said, "Let's shoot the thirty-ought-six." He said, "Let's shoot the oak tree," which was on the other side of some barbed wire, on some land owned by that ob-gyn who later in life came out of the closet and had an article written about his partner and him in *Southern Living*. This was a man who collected rare animals—he had two albino deer when we moved into the subdivision that fronted his property—and one time had this great Irish terrier dog named Courtney who used to come over to our house, through the fence, daily. Courtney ended up destroying the ob-gyn's wife's Mercedes' interior, he gave the dog to a family he knew way over in Saluda, some thirty miles away, and a week later Courtney showed up at our house, skinny, cut up, tick-infested, and betangled with briars. My father took the dog to the Greenwood Humane Society, talked to a man named Mr. E.L. Caldecott, explained the situation, and Mr. Caldecott said, "The dog's yours, then."

For what it's worth, Courtney could smile on demand. If a person said, "Smile, Courtney!" she'd dip her head, bare her teeth, and make a noise out of her nostrils not unlike an asthmatic. She'd bob her head while smiling, too, as if doing an impression of a trick horse on par with Mr. Ed. She also thought it necessary to play Tag every time she went outside without a leash. We kept Courtney the entire time we had my big white dog Gypsy — I'd found her beneath a bus at the Greenwood County Airport one afternoon. She, too, was covered with ticks when I went back to get her. She feared my father's cane for the longest time, then became, with Courtney, his best friend.

So my father took me outside the house with a rifle used to shoot elephants, and I said, "This is going to backfire and hurt me."

He said, "Back up and put your shoulder to the house. Then it won't backfire."

When I pulled the trigger, it felt like my shoulder ricocheted somewhere back inside the house, all the way to the fireplace. I don't know if I hit the tree. I started crying. I went, "Owwwww," and dropped the gun.

My father said, "Don't believe nothing your dad tells you." Great advice.

Anyway, on those five-dollar-an-hour days, we'd work on the already-perfect splitting machine, then go out back and shoot the pistol into a roll of butcher paper. I have no clue why my father kept butcher paper around his shop.

Aside: One time he had Courtney with him

at work. This guy, Dale Bobo—whom I went to school with—lived a couple doors down, facing the Memorial Gardens where my father's buried. Dale Bobo might've been twenty years old in twelfth grade, and he lived alone, having moved out of his parents' house at some point.

Dale Bobo owned a pit bull, back before pit bulls were all the rage among inner-city youths and redneck dogfighters. His pit bull attacked Courtney. My father limped out of his shop, fired the .22 in the ground, Courtney took off running, and the bullet ricocheted off a rock and killed Dale Bobo's dog. My father buried it in the woods. Courtney remained missing for a few days before showing back up, again briar-covered and scraped. A number of years went by. I ran into Dale Bobo in a bar. He said, "Listen, I know your daddy killed Precious." He said, "I forgive him."

I had to think back. First, I was in a bar. Two, maybe I'd undergone a lot of experiences since whenever all that happened. Of course I said, "I don't think so."

We'd shoot the pistol, then my father would say, "It's about time for coffee," and we'd drive over to Godfrey's Market.

Godfrey's Market is no longer with us, unfortunately. The building's there—a new building, after a fire damaged the original hundred-year-old structure back on February 13, 2002—but the ownership's changed twice. In the old days, Frank and Pete Godfrey, brothers, ran the store. They sold feed and seed. They sold Little Debbies snack cakes. In July, one could buy the best hash there—eating, not smoking, hash. They cured their own country hams, which set out on display. Cigarettes, candy, bread, canned meat. Work gloves, hoes, sling blades, gasoline. But the best part about Godfrey's Market—and what lawyers, doctors, unemployed ne'er-do-wells, teachers, truck drivers, pulpwooders, farmers, and college students showed up for daily—took place in the kitchen, and back behind the glass display cases. Fresh hamburgers, fresh sausage patties, fresh chicken, fresh ham sandwiches. Everything not dead more than twenty-four hours, it seemed.

The Godfreys kept people's accounts on little flip-through notebooks, and at the beginning of each month—or when people felt flushed with money—customers paid up, no interest added. Rich and poor, Black and White, men and women and children. The latest wingtips, standing next to clay-covered logging boots, standing next to high heels, standing next to rubber boots spattered with cow manure.

The general store attracted a handful of those so unfortunately maimed they probably shied from going into downtown Greenwood. I cannot count on both hands how many men I met over a ten-year period who no longer owned bottom jaws, or didn't possess eyes, the result of a self-inflicted mis-aimed pistol or shotgun during a low point in their lives. It didn't keep them from trying to talk non-stop to everyone in that indecipherable language of the once-suicidal. I learned to nod, stare at the ground, and look occupied because of Godfrey's Market.

My father and I would go straight to the back of the store and get seats next to a wooden butcher block that stood six feet wide and six feet deep. More often than not Pete Godfrey would haul a dead pig onto it, and start to cutting. There was a sausage grinder off to the side, too, and while my father and I drank coffee, and ate cheeseburgers, the constant farting sound of grinding sausage filled our ears. While we ate sausage patties bigger than a large man's palm, with tomatoes and mayonnaise and cheese, served on hamburger rolls, Pete or Frank whipped butcher knives around, taking time out only to sharpen those blades on whetstones and strops gathered from Hades. I never took a Music Appreciation class in college, because maybe I understood Mozart and Shostakovich could never compose anything on par with stropped knives fiddling behind a sausage grinder.

At the end of the day — we'd go back, put the splitting machine back together, run a strip of calfskin through it, find out that the blade, sure enough, didn't have a little dink — my father would pull into the carport. I'd look at my watch. "Eight hours," I'd say. "Forty bucks."

He'd hand me a five dollar bill. "You worked for one."

WHY WE DON'T
PLAY CHESS

OVER THE LAST eleven years, a variety of stray dogs have moved in with Glenda and me, out here in the country, in the middle of nowhere South Carolina. Between twenty and fifty miles away is a long string of new suburbia, along Interstate 85, and I can only surmise those hammerheads living out that way bring their unwanted animals and dump them nearby. Across from our house stands about five hundred acres of tree farm, and at night we can hear dogs running, yelping, howling, and usually finding our driveway soon thereafter. At this moment we have ten dogs, all mixed breeds. Nutmeg had to be put down last month, and is buried in the fenced-in backyard beside Kelly, Lucy, and a good half-dozen unknown and nameless dogs found dead in our front yard, where other hammerheads—those who drive 60 miles an hour down two-lane Hester Store Road each morning in order to work at the new factories along I-85—didn't stop after hitting what tree farm dogs hadn't made it to home base, i.e., here.

I should mention that we haven't kept every dog that came along, either. My mother has an ex-feral dog named Maggie. Various friends, neighbors, and veterinarians have taken over dogs. And I've gone out more than a few times to find some non-blinking and skittish cur, called her toward me, then had her barrel back into the tree farm.

Oh, it's an exciting life. It keeps us busy, for one, and when Glenda and I have to take off for one reason or another I like to think we're offering a valuable lesson to our dog-sitters—usually students or ex-students—dog psychology. And for anyone who says the younger generation never exercises their collective minds, let me say that my feeding instructions, at the very least, have more possible plot twists than one of those old, old chess matches played between Russian grand masters.

My dog River, aged eleven and coyote-looking, can eat in any room in the house. But she must eat alone. River's the queen of the entire operation, an alpha dog inside and out. She has never attacked one of the other dogs, nor has she bitten one. But she bares her teeth and lets out growls similar to bad bedsprings, over and over. She looks peripherally, always. If another dog doesn't finish his or her meal, River will forever gladly stick her head in the bowl and eat. Then she'll get sick later on that night.

Joan kind of looks like a yellow Lab, and she's the alpha dog outside when River's not present. Joan rarely comes inside, as a matter of fact, and stays in a 20x40-foot chain-link pen, which leads into a mostly empty 12 x 20 storage shed. Joan shares the facility with Hershey, a brown Weimaraner-looking dog who can leap the chain-link fence. So he's on a long lead, tied to the trunk of a peach tree. Hershey can still leap over the fence, and come out into the yard about another fifteen feet. And he does so in order to eat, seeing Joan will bully him and take his food. If let loose and unsupervised, Hershey digs holes the size of bomb shelters.

Inklet looks like a black Lab, and she spends most of her day in Glenda's clay studio, with Ann, who is mostly Pit Bull. Ann owns fused back legs, and hops. Between Joan, Hershey, Inklet, and Ann, you could count about a dozen teeth. All of them have a hankering for immature peaches that fall off the trees in the backyard, and over the years they have ground their teeth to little nubs.

Inklet eats slowly; Ann doesn't. The two can eat together, but Ann needs to go outside beforehand because she'll urinate in her bowl directly after eating, so that nobody else will touch her dining area. At least that's my theory. Hershey does the same thing, on the other side of the chain-link fence, right before jumping back to be with Joan when all of the inside dogs get let out, ready to corner poor Hershey, seeing as he seems to be the low dog.

Nick is fairly new, not a year old, a black, black, sleek mostly Pointer. He still eats like a wild dog. If he eats in the company of the other dogs, he'll bolt down his food, get an odd look on his face, regurgitate, and then make me walk back out of the room not feeling so well myself. So Nick needs to eat on the back patio, only if Hershey's done with his food.

It's important to know, too, that Glenda and

I got tired of walking all of these dogs on leashes each morning, and she splurged to fence in an acre out back with a 6-foot-high privacy fence, which surrounds the pen, the barn, the fenced-in raised-bed gardens (every one of our dogs thinks that tennis balls grow on tomato plants) and so on.

Charlie, who lived in our monkey grass one winter for a couple weeks before coming in, looks like a miniature Spaniel. He barely eats a cup of dog food a day. But he'll fight to the death if anyone comes near his bowl. Marty has an underbite that could get him a job as a soup ladle at any fancy French restaurant. The vet said he could be made up of about eight different breeds. Marty can eat with Charlie, if and only if their bowls are on opposite sides of the kitchen. Stella kind of looks like a miniature River, and she's been known to bare teeth and sink them in if another dog happens by. She can eat in the kitchen, too, if Glenda or I stand there; otherwise, she eats in the hallway.

Dooley's about a hundred pounds of white-and-liver-freckled, manic, goofy off-bird dog. He showed up one winter morning, practically crawling across the front yard, as submissive as he could be. But he has the personality of an old drunk: If he's not telling the other dogs how much he loves them — inviting them over to share his bowl — then he's going for the jugular. Dooley must eat alone in what used to be a laundry room.

Stella, Marty, and Charlie cannot eat in my workroom because they're small, and the covered cat litter box is back here, and they think it's an hors d'oeuvre tray. Dooley can never eat outside because he'll see a carpenter bee and chase it forever. When any of the dogs are feeling puny and have lost their appetite for dry dog food—and we get them those special diet bags, for old dogs, dogs with bad joints, psychotic dogs—then we have to feed them a mixture of wet food and table scraps. For the most part our dogs are never finicky; a good ex-tree-farm-living stray dog will take dry food over field mice, snakes, and roadkill, I'm thinking.

If the dogs leave food in their bowls, though, it must be picked up soon thereafter, for Herb the cat—also a stray, and mostly a dog—has an appetite for their food. Or maybe he only wants them to think he's really boss.

If it's thundering, Dooley, Inklet, Ann, Joan, and Hershey won't eat at all, and need to be taken one at a time to a closed-door bathroom. If it's that spring forward or fall back day and we change the clocks, it goofs up everybody involved. If it's dead winter, Glenda and I go through this routine in the morning and afternoon, though with half as much food.

On any given day, any one of our dogs—aged ten months to maybe twelve years old—could change his or her mind as to what he or she wants. At any time, I know, one of the dogs could become a bishop and move as diagonally as he or she wanted. Any one of the dogs could evolve into a rook, and move forward, backward, or sideways, in regard to food distribution and place setting. These ex-strays are never pawns. They do not move forward one square at a time.

Clearly — if I had the time or wherewithal — if I played chess, half of my dogs would mistake the pieces or pawns for stylized peach pits. And they would gnaw and growl and check each other's distance, and wag their tails like men in a park, thinking ten moves ahead.

THE REAL VALUE OF
BOOK REPORTS

ALTHOUGH I THOUGHT of myself as a writer only when I ran in the mornings, or while watching Henry Gibson recite those poems on *Laugh-In*, I guess I began writing fiction in the tenth grade for a woman named Mrs. Jones who might've been the worst English teacher of all time. This woman taught me regular, plain Tenth Grade English. I wasn't in some kind of AP class, or even college prep. I don't remember any of my friends ever sweating over incredibly-difficult classes in the language arts, sciences, or math, so maybe those options weren't available in the mid-Seventies. I'm betting they were, and that I just didn't quite qualify. In elementary school I scored in the top 98% when it came time for that annual Iowa Basic Skills tests, but beginning in about the seventh grade something happened to me, maybe I got bored, maybe a few of those early concussions added up, I don't know. I started making Cs in classes I thought boring, or—in the case of algebra/geometry/algebra II/every freaking science—beyond my mental abilities.

Mrs. Jones was an African-American woman married to a Pentecostal minister. If her speech pattern were an animal, she'd've been a member of the sloth family, more than likely. She wore her hair in a tight black-and-gray bun, and rarely blinked her sleepy eyes. Molasses could beat her in a race to the door.

For no reason that anyone of us could figure out, one day she announced, "There are ghosts. Oftentimes when my husband and I drive at night down to the low country, we see ghosts traveling beside the car." I wondered if she merely caught her reflection in the passenger side window, maybe caused by the light off her preacher husband's glow-in-the-dark crucifix perched on his lapel.

Part of the curriculum involved everyone standing up in front of class to give oral book reports about every other week. I don't remember taking a test in this class, or reading any kind of assigned text, though I'm sure we did. All the way through high school I underwent what's now known, probably, as "panic attacks," when it came to having to speak in front of a group of people. My voice quavered, I breathed way too quick and audibly, and my face remained bright red whenever I had to give a book report.

Aside: One time back in the ninth grade, when I was some kind of student council representative—my friend Victor Gwinn, who grew up in an orphanage, happened to be president—I had to read, aloud, into a microphone with the entire student body in the gymnasium, a longish "Christmas poem" written in rhymed couplets. Understand I didn't write this execrable thing. And luckily I didn't have to memorize it. But it was long.

My mother understood how nervous I became, so she gave me a "special pill." For someone so worried about marijuana leading to heroin, she sure seemed able to provide "special pills" whenever I needed one. I now realize this might've been a Valium, or whatever Valium might've been called in 1972.

Victor Gwinn suffered from the same malady as I. This entire Northside Junior High Christmas Production would air on one of the public access channels no one watched, unless they needed information on garbage pick-up days, or the time and temperature, or who to call should a colony of bats swoop down and block a major intersection. Victor got up to the microphone, mumbled something, then, louder than normal, said, "And now George Singleton will read us a Christmas prayer."

Prayer! The entire student body, teachers, staff, and parents bowed their heads. My voice didn't waver like someone trying to conduct a conversation while aboard a hovercraft. I wondered what everyone thought, though, when I went into something that came off like "Christmas is that time of year/When thoughts of Jesus do not veer//We love our friends, and even strangers/Because of a baby born in a manger..."

I got into it. I enunciated every syllable. Had I been reading this thing post-1990 I would've probably added some arm movements and gone all Snoop Dogg on the thing. It must've lasted ten minutes—like the Christmas equivalent of *The Wasteland*.

My parents and I turned on the public

access network later on—like a week later—and watched. My voice didn't waver, but that pill evidently gave me some kind of rubber-leg syndrome. It looked like a white Sammy Davis, Jr. read the thing. Evidently James Brown turned on public access from all the way down in Augusta, Georgia, and that's where he learned some of his moves. Michael Jackson might've incorporated some of those Moon Walk slides after honing in on my copyright-worthy Slinky-leg visuals. Whoever invented the crazy inflatable advertising air dancer, seen normally flopping out of control at used car lots, evidently turned on public access 69 back then, too.

But back to Mrs. Jones: I took the class during what must've been a 90-minute period, with a lunch break in between. A high-pitched noise came on over the intercom about every ten or fifteen minutes, so different floors and different buildings could shuffle off to the lunch room. Some classes—this was one of them—met for thirty minutes, then students went to lunch, then they returned for twenty minutes. I don't have an advanced degree in Education, but it seems to me this break wasn't the most beneficial for the learning process. Hell, it took this woman fifteen minutes to call the roll. Then someone might give a book report. Then lunch, then two book reports.

After every book report—and I know I'm prone to exaggeration, but this ain't one of those times—Mrs. Jones said, "I have read that book and, yes, it is a very fine book, a very fine book."

We might not have been the hardiest stalks in the cornfield, but my classmates and I figured there was no way for our teacher to have read every book ever shoved onto our school library's shelves.

So we started making them up.

"For my book report, I'm going to talk about Frank Shorter's *Long Vacation with the Hidden Tribe,*" I might've said, hoping that Mrs. Jones didn't recognize the winner of the marathon in the 1972 Olympics. "It's about this boy, named Frank, who gets lost while camping with his parents up in the Appalachian Mountains. They go looking for him, and after a couple weeks they figure a bear must've gotten him. Anyway, forest rangers come in, you know, and then they say there's no hope, and then Frank Shorter's parents are all sad and return home from their vacation. Well, Frank isn't dead. He strayed from the path, and then he got turned around, and then he met up with some Indians from a tribe no one knew even existed—a tribe of Cherokees who hid a long time ago so as not to be included in the Trail of Tears." I'd go on and on, my voice making that noise, my eyes welling up, my face so red that airplane pilots changed their flight patterns in order to land at the next closest county airport instead of the one a few miles from my high school. "Finally, the Indians teach Frank Shorter all about their way of life, and then a scout helps him get home only after Frank promises to tell the story of the Hidden Tribe. The end." Oh, there in the middle I'd go into made-up details about Frank's looks, or about his sister, or about his pipe-smoking father. I learned the best lies told contain a thousand details. Who'd make up such a thing about the mother's bunions, and how hiking had always been difficult for her, and that's why Frank got ahead of his family, then lost?"

"I have read that book and, yes, it is a very fine book, a very fine book," Mrs. Jones would say. Then the bell went *Eeeeeeeeeeek!* "Everyone go to lunch."

So one day in class, not much longer after Mrs. Jones found it necessary to offer up her low country ghost population belief, I got a couple conspirators together and laid out some plans. After she finally got through with the roll I said, "Ms. Jones, do you believe that dreams come true? I mean, like you have a dream at night, and then that same thing happens in real life?"

She nodded on pace with how a cartoon tortoise nods. She said, "I know they do. I've had very many of my dreams come true."

Yes, I thought. "Last night I had a dream that we were going to have an earthquake today, right at about twenty till one."

Mrs. Jones stared at me, didn't smile, didn't blink, and said, "Well, it might could happen."

One of those godawful tones went off at 12:40. It went off, and this kid named Chuck, and a young woman named Laura, and maybe a half-dozen other kids started shaking our desks like we suffered from the worst palsy ever. Chuck, in front of me, kicked an empty desk hard, and it rammed into Mrs. Jones's desk. He yelled out, "It's that earthquake George was talking about!"

This was on the third floor, so I'm sure the class beneath us wondered what the hell happened. Mrs. Jones clapped her hands hard and yelled out, "Class! Class!" and then—again, no exaggeration—said, "Goddamn it class, stop it!"

We did stop. And we all said, "Ooooooohhhhh," for she was the wife of a pentecostal minister who shouldn't say "goddamn."

I know I've never been the most sympathetic person in the world at times, but I felt bad, bad, bad about this. I felt terrible. I don't know for sure, but my next book report might've been on an actual YA novel.

She won, though. I asked Mrs. Jones one time, "Where does that apostrophe go in the word 'didn't'? Is it between the *en* and the *tee*, or the *dee* and the *en*?"

She said, "It don't matter."

Or she said, "It do'nt matter," I'll never know.

She also pronounced "hyperbole" as "hyper bowl."

GAR

I CAN BARELY SWIM. I never learned how to swim like normal people, who can somehow exhale their breaths under water, turn their heads, breathe in, and so on, all the while windmilling their arms in an effortless manner. Early on I took swimming lessons — like at the age of four or five, before we moved to South Carolina. And I could go from one end of an Olympic-sized pool to the other without taking a breath, my head face down in the water. I could dog paddle. I could pull off an average backstroke, I guess. But when it came to the Australian crawl, I kept my head out of the water and thrashed around mercilessly. Thalidomide babies could beat me in a race that involved going across a pool and back. Stephen Hawking could beat me. My body won't even float, really — I need to kick my feet like crazy just to keep my head above the surface. Stephen Hawking in his wheelchair could float better than I.

So it kind of surprised my parents when I came home from the last day of driving the garbage truck — that beautification department gig for high school and college students lasted from June first until mid-August only — and announced that, until I had to return for my senior year in college, I'd be working as a lifeguard down at Lake Greenwood State Park. "You can't even swim!" my mother said, bent over laughing.

My father said, "Don't think I'm not going to check up on you. Don't think you're so smart." He figured that I'd just get up every morning and drive around for eight hours, then return home, so I wouldn't have to work for him, tearing down perfectly-operating machinery, leaving the parts scattered about, shooting his pistol at makeshift targets, then sitting around Godfrey's Market for the rest of the day.

My friend Paul Borick could swim, as could his brothers Jim and Kenny. They got jobs down at the state park, which even furnished them with a cabin two coves over from the swimming area. Paul went to the University of Tennessee, which started classes mid-September, as did Furman, where I went. Jim and Kenny attended normal state colleges that began each semester on or about the fifteenth of August.

The state park's swimming area remained open until the weekend after Labor Day.

"I talked Willie T. into hiring you on, if you want it," Paul said to me.

Willie T. worked for the park ranger. I knew him. We had stood side by side in front of a magistrate in early June.

One Saturday I drove over to the Borick brothers' cabin. I took out my special bought-in-France notebook, in order to work on what would end up being my first piece of fiction, a horrible 450 page novel.

I sat down at the picnic table outside of the cabin, with my pen, my notebook, and a quart of

Jim Beam, plus a regular drinking glass, filched from a Holiday Inn bathroom. Boy oh boy. This was the life, being a writer! I stared off across the lake. I counted boats. I looked to where fish surfaced. I chased a northern brown water snake.

I drank from my Jim Beam, and waved to people. I mixed the bourbon with Coke. I ran out of ice and didn't care. I wondered where I might be able to buy a fedora. I smoked two cigarettes at a time, and made a big production out of looking tortured while blowing smoke rings. I thought about Native Americans, their smoke signals, then quit—what would happen if I accidentally called *help* and a tribe of warriors showed up? I giggled to myself. I thought up punk songs that involved Opie Taylor. I wrote down sentences not unlike what the Billy Crystal character writes ("The night was hot,""The night was moist," "The night was humid," "The night was foggy") in that movie about a writer that would come out eight years later. Because I had the novel set in France, I probably went through stuff like "The night was noir" or "The night was not magnifique." I got up and looked inside one of those wooden birdhouses with the round hole and peg in front, got out an old nest, and brought it to the picnic table. I gathered pine needles nearby, and tried to construct a nest as if I had the genetic make-up of an ancient Gullah basket weaver.

And then Willie T. showed up, parked his pickup, and ambled down my way. I said, "I'm not trespassing or anything. Nothing to worry about here. I'm a friend of Paul's."

He looked like a really dark Smokey Bear,

wearing that same hat and all. He said, "Uh-huh."

I probably said, "I'm going to be a writer!" like an idiot.

He picked up my Jim Beam and said, "Ain't no alcohol allowed inside the park."

I said, "I didn't know."

I swear to god he said, "You being a writer, seems like you could read that big sign there at the entrance of the park. No alcohol."

He wrote me up a ticket. He took the bottle away. He said, "You been so cooperative, I'll ask the judge to be light on you."

I said, "Thanks."

So I ended up having to appear in magistrate's court a few weeks later, and Willie T. was there. The judge called my name, and I approached his desk. Willie T. came along. Willie T. said, "Your honor," and listed out the entire story pretty much like I just wrote it out, except his not knowing exactly what I did not writing. And he said, "Mr. Singleton made an honest mistake, I believe, and he was very agreeable. He didn't offer no trouble at all."

The magistrate said to me, "Do you have anything to say?"

I said, "I knew it was going to be a bad day, getting caught at the very first drink."

He said, "What time was it?"

"About eight in the morning," I said, as a joke, being funny, like all beginning writers should be.

The magistrate banged his gavel and fined me the maximum amount, which was something like $75, as I remember.

Two months later I arrived at the state

park, and said hey to Willie T., and explained that I didn't have a lifeguard certificate. I didn't mention I could barely swim. He said, "Well, we need someone out here. Listen, if anyone shows up looking official like, just start picking up litter."

Here's the scene: There was the standard-issue lifeguard stand on a fake beach of white sand. The swimming area was cordoned off with those little floats and ski rope. I'd say that it was a good two acres in area. Way out in the lake was a dock, and a wooden diving board. While one lifeguard sat under the umbrellaed stand, another sat out there on the dock. A third worked the snack bar. Every hour, the three workers rotated. I don't remember the third person whatsoever. I know this: gar fish circled that dock, non-stop. I'm talking three-foot garfish, their fins above the water, those little razor teeth smiling. They're like freshwater possums, if you ask me.

I could swim out to that dock maybe the first and second time—starting off with a crawl, ending in a dog paddle—but there toward the end of the day I had to paddle out in a canoe, tie it to the dock, and hope some little kid jumping into a circle of garfish didn't freak out and go under. I yelled at kids not to venture out beyond my reach on the wooden platform.

No one drowned.

Ha ha ha ha ha.

I went back to college, not knowing how I had little talent in a number of areas.

THE GREAT SINGLETINI

O NE DAY, my father and I drove aimlessly around town. We stopped at the post office and saw Mr. Neil Cost, the turkey-call carver. We went by the Try Me restaurant for fried chicken, and said hey to Little David. Nothing important seemed to be going on. We drove by to see Mr. Beasley, who—in his law office—took on a different persona, that of being a counselor of the law, not a fun-loving *bon vivant* fond of bourbon. He understood, intuitively, Carl Jung's notion of social masks. We drove around in my grandmother's Galaxie, part of the deal when she left for San Francisco.

I had given my father *On the Road*, by Kerouac. This must've been right before my father got sick. This occurred right before his idiot primary care doctor—a guy named McKinney (a man I, later, accosted in the hallway of the hospital and threatened, calling him a quack)—went from saying my father suffered from asthma, then bronchitis, then walking pneumonia, then pneumonia before I returned home, found my father barely able to talk, found him a great internist, and so on.

My father read *On the Road,* and he said, "Those guys were fucking bums."

I said, "I kind of like that novel."

121

"All they do is take drugs, drink, tell stories, and drive around."

He went down highway 10, toward McCormick, then turned around at Connie Maxwell Children's Home. He drove like a gangsta, leaned way back, one hand holding the steering wheel.

I said, "Dad."

"Goddamn it, I wasn't nothing like that."

"Double negative," I said.

He gritted his teeth in the same manner I find myself doing, more often than I wish, these days. I always said I never wanted to grow up and be like my father, but good god, there's something to that DNA: I wake up at 4:30. If I go to bed at nine, I wake up at 4:30, and if I go to bed at two in the morning I wake up at 4:30. I make sure everyone knows I'm up, and that they should be up; I have exactly zero patience for fools; I question authority on a minute-by-minute basis, and so on. I don't like pain killers though, unless it comes to Goody's Powders and bourbon.

Aside: I don't know when HBO came around, but we had it at my parents' house in 1980 or thereabouts. *The Great Santini* came on. My mother and I watched it. I was either right at the end of college, or my first year out, visiting home from my wonderful dishwashing at Steak and Ale/warehouse-working at Budweiser jobs up in Greenville. I am sure it was I who said, "That Santini guy's a little bit like Dad."

A week went by. *The Great Santini* came back on. My father sat in his clunky, green cloth, not-easy-to-unrecline-from recliner. We watched for about thirty minutes, when my father raised his legs as best he could in order to make a loud exit from the chair. He yelled, "I'm not like that guy!"

My mother sat in her chair. I sat on the couch, with Gypsy beside me.

"Who said you were like that guy? We didn't say anything," I said.

"I know what you were thinking, goddamn it!" my father said, barreling out of the room, limping, on his way to the guest bedroom.

My mother and I waited for him to be down the hallway before we both broke out laughing.

Twenty-four years later I stood in a bar in Atlanta, during a book conference. Pat Conroy walked up. He didn't know me. I said, "Hey, Mr. Conroy." I introduced myself, then told the story of *The Great Santini* on TV. I said, "We kind of called my father 'The Great Singletini' after that episode."

Mr. Conroy held his head sideways, inched one side of his lips upward, and said, "Man, I'm sorry. I know."

Kind of an aside: The next day, the *Atlanta Journal-Constitution* ran a full page Sunday edition glowing review of my linked collection of stories *Why Dogs Chase Cars.* I was in my hotel room, packing up, when my buddy Ron Rash came by and said, "Pat Conroy's down in the restaurant. He wants to talk to you."

I came down to find Mr. Conroy there, in the middle of a crowded Sunday brunch crowd, seated with his lovely wife Cassandra King. He had that *Book Review* section of the newspaper, folded, up in the air. "Look at you, look at you!" he bellowed. "Mr. Big! Yesterday you were shit on my shoe, and tomorrow you'll be shit on my shoe, but right now, you're Mr. Big!" He was kind of deaf at this point—by "kind of," I mean "really hard of hearing." So he wasn't aware his booming voice might divert jets from over at Hartsfield International Airport. Everyone at the hotel restaurant turned around.

Cassandra said, "Pat."

I kind of saw my father in Mr. Conroy's face. I broke out into a smile. I said, "Thanks. Hey, why're you here? You're pushing some kind of cookbook you wrote, right?"

"You got me!" he said. "Damn, son, you got me!"

I sat down, I ordered coffee, and we started talking about the long, long rivalry between Furman, where I went to college, and the Citadel, where he graduated. We gave each other shit. We laughed. We pointed in each other's face. He gave me his telephone number and said to call him at any time, should I want to wager about who'd win the next Furman-Citadel football or basketball game. Cassandra said to me out of the side of her mouth, "It won't matter. You'll call, and he won't hear the phone ring."

What a great, generous man, Conroy.

My father and I kept driving around on this one day, until we got behind a man, stopped at a red light, his phone to his ear. Again, this might've been 1980. This was not a time for cell phones. I'm sure car phones existed, but they weren't hard to miss, what with the twelve-foot whip antennae swinging behind the car like the meanest wasp stingers ever.

This man—a very, very successful man later on—held a regular landline telephone to his ear, pretending to talk to someone, the gyred cord falling down somewhere between his knees. Everyone knew about his need to look important. My father said, "Peckerhead." When he wasn't saying "counterdicting," he was saying "peckerhead." He liked to throw in an "indubitably" whenever possible, too.

He said, "Trying to look like he's rich and important."

And then we followed the man, a man who later started up a company that provides Bi-Lo, Publix, and Ingles with pimento cheese shrimp dip, a man who started up a restaurant on Lake Greenwood that may or may not have finally run the Panorama out of business, for all I know.

We followed close behind the guy, down Durst, up Cambridge, down Montague, over to Laurel, finally to a convenience store where the man needed gasoline.

My father got out of the car. He walked up to this guy's driver's side. He said, "Hey, buddy, I noticed you talking on the phone. I really need to call my wife and ask her what we need at the grocery store. I forgot to bring the list."

The man didn't get out. I sat in my father's car like an idiot. I could hear everything, though—seeing as the windows were down because the air conditioner didn't work.

"Let me just borrow your phone a second. I'll give you money for your time," my father said, his elbow on the roof of this man's sedan.

The man—and think about it, if you ever buy pimento cheese shrimp dip at the grocery store—started up his engine and took off.

Later, I said, "That guy's a peckerhead."

My father—and I'm not making any of this up—said, "Indubitably."

AN ODE TO
HANGOVER CURES

HANGOVER THEORISTS—evidently there are but a few professionally, but a whole crash of them working nonstop on an amateur basis—don't talk much about congeners and cytokines, at least not publicly. But anyone who has ever ingested more than 1.5 ounces of good bourbon per hour knows he or she will suffer the classic symptoms right about daybreak: inflammation of the head, queasy stomach, and slight tremulousness. Personally, I don't get that 1.5 ounces per hour quota. Did a scientist make a typo? Did Dr. Moderation really mean 5.1 ounces per hour?

Here in South Carolina, where the hangovers come quickly and often, the cures are mind-numbing and questionable. Every good booze glutton has probably tried the standbys: two gallons of water, enough Goody's Powder sleeves to construct a life-size origami swan, Krystal hamburgers, hair of the dog, and a slew of over-the-counter, sure-fire remedies usually sold next to condoms, batteries, playing cards, and scratch tickets at the local convenience store.

What I suggest may only work on me, but it works. Without trudging through a stream of techno-babble involving dilated blood vessels and acetaldehyde, let me leave you with these words: embrace the endorphin-inducing hot peppers.

In the past—yeah, yeah, yeah, I just went through rehab, so trust me I'm clear-headed and slightly rational on the following recipe—I started my day with what I call Poor Man's Pâté Surprise. I minced a can of Vienna sausages as fine as possible (a blender would work best, but remember, the damn noise could kill you) and threw them into a blue-speckled, enamelware mixing bowl. I think it's called "splatterware," which is appropriate. Then, recklessly and without rubber gloves, I minced one medium jalapeño and one orange habanero, then threw them on top of the Viennas, seeds and all. During particularly vile, rabid, tenacious hangovers, I always hoped that the pepper seeds would lodge in my intestinal tract, cause diverticulitis, and kill me.

Then I added about two tablespoons of Duke's mayo, two squirts of plain French's yellow mustard, and a couple teaspoons of sweet-pickle relish. I hand-whipped the concoction with a wooden spoon and served it atop saltine crackers, or between two slices of white Sunbeam bread. I never officially recorded the outcome, but it seemed as if my hands would start burning uncontrollably about the same time I could see again through the tears. Granted, my hangover remedy might be on the same level as a guy who bangs his thumb with a hammer so he forgets about his gout, but what the hell. By the time I knew what was going on, my headache had disappeared.

I should also add to any animal lovers out there that my Poor Man's Pâté Surprise, minus the peppers, has cured more than a few of my dogs when they scrawnied away during hot summer months and wouldn't eat regular chow.

I discovered another hangover cure that might work best for upwardly mobile people living in nice neighborhoods without a Vienna sausage aisle in their grocery store.

Take two catfish fillets and place them in a shallow, buttered, borosilicate glass pan, better known as Pyrex cookware. Sprinkle grated cheese on the fish. Cover the cheese with, again, diced jalapeños and habaneros. Cover the peppers with bread crumbs, then another layer of fillets.

Sometimes I grated more cheese — I preferred hoop cheese, but I'm sure some kind of high-priced and fancy Havarti, Gouda, or Edam might work — and added more bread crumbs. I baked the catfish at around 400 degrees for maybe fifteen minutes, depending on the thickness of the fillets. Then I pulled out the pan and carefully drained into a mixing bowl the fish water that had mysteriously accumulated.

It was important to keep the fish water, as I'll explain later.

Then I slid the pan back in the oven for about another five minutes. During this time, I made not-from-scratch hollandaise sauce, which I drizzled over the fish loaf after it cooled somewhat. Now, I'll admit, sometimes this particular hangover cure didn't quite work. For the most part — minus the butter, cheese, and hollandaise sauce—it seemed about as healthy as a shot of B12. If my hangover didn't go away by the time I finished off about a four-by-four-inch square, there was one more step.

I went back to my pantry—or closet, file cabinet, Charles Chips canister, suitcase, roof gutter, dog food bin, bookcase, et cetera—pulled out a bottle of vodka or bourbon, poured about a jigger into the cooling fish water, and chugged it down. A little hair of the dog and scale of the catfish pretty much relieved me of any discomfort. This little step worked amazingly well for those who suffered from upset stomachs.

Let me reiterate that I only speak of what worked for me. I have no scientific evidence, but it seems to me that the blood vessels may actually constrict, despite the theories, and if so, there's nothing like a good, fatty Vienna sausage to ramrod those veins back into viable thoroughfares. The hot peppers, I'm certain, send out endorphins so fast that even a broken hip might feel like nothing more than a pulled groin.

Oddly, since the rehab stint, I've noticed how my knees, lower back, neck, and temples hurt pretty much continuously. I'm thinking I might should go back to my old midmorning ways, pop those Vienna tops more often, and dice peppers like there's no tomorrow.

HOW TO WRITE STORIES, LOSE WEIGHT, CLEAN UP THE ENVIRONMENT, AND MAKE $1,000,000

THIS PLAN WILL WORK if and only if the writer-to-be is, say, twenty-five years old and intends to live another fifty years. But it's fun to play, even if you start at age thirty or forty. Maybe it'll give you the incentive to live past ninety.

DAY ONE

Wake up early and sit in front of the computer, or open up a nice Mead composition notebook. It doesn't matter. I will assume you know what a short story is—basically a 5,000 word piece of fiction with a recognizable beginning, middle, and end that involves a protagonist trying to best an antagonist. There will be rising action, conflict, dialogue, and maybe even a beautiful, lyrical passage shoved somewhere in the middle —when you weren't quite sure where the story was headed.

On the first day, put two characters in an uncomfortable situation. Maybe you're writing about the time you were sixteen years old and buying condoms, and your boyfriend or girlfriend's mother walked up behind you. That's pretty awkward, if you ask me. This is fiction, though, so you need to make up some crap. Make the mother limp, too, for instance. Have her holding a package of bunion pads.

Anyway, write 1,000 words on that first day.

Now go out—this will work if and only if you live out in the country, in a state that doesn't offer a nickel for cans, seeing as no one in those states throws nickels out the open car window, I doubt, like they do where I live in South Carolina—with a plastic trash bag and pick up at least fifty aluminum cans. This might take as much as a quarter mile of walking.

Come back home and place the cans upright. Stomp on them. This will reduce space. Throw the cans in some kind of container with a top— a rubber garbage can, for instance. If you live in an apartment complex, make sure that your neighbors don't snoop around and steal your cans. Wait. You live in the country. You live in a place like South Carolina. Maybe I should've mentioned you might be living in a trailer.

Anyway, put up the cans. Start thinking about tomorrow.

DAY TWO

Reread your first 1,000 words. Rewrite. If you chose to write in a notebook, type up the rewrite on a computer. I'm not going to mention this again.

Make sure your characters' names didn't change somewhere in the middle. Pick right up where you left off, and add another 1,000 words. Then go out and gather another fifty cans, which might take you as much as a half-mile of walking. Stomp. Add to the first batch.

DAY THREE

Reread your first 2,000 words. Rewrite. Write another 1,000. Go out on that walk and retrieve fifty cans, which might take three-quarters of a mile. Don't forget to wash your hands when you get home. I should've mentioned that earlier, too. Stomp and add to the first two days' batch.

DAY FOUR

Reread your first 3,000 words. Rewrite. Write another 1,000 words. Go walk a mile and pick up fifty cans. Stomp them when you get home. Make a note to change the antagonist's name, because you don't want to get sued later on in life by people who don't have the tenacity to become famous, rich, skinny, and environmentally-conscious in the old-fashioned, difficult way. Add your cans into the bin and realize that you've picked up two hundred aluminum cans already. Good job. You're doing your part. If you want to celebrate, make sure to drink beer out of a can so you can add it to your collection.

DAY FIVE

Reread your first 4,000 words. Rewrite. Write another 1,000 words. Finish up that first draft of your story. You've probably been thinking up possible titles while taking your aluminum-gathering walks, so make a decision. First off, ditch the first two or three titles that come into your mind. One of them will probably be some-thing like "The Lesson." One of them might be

"Good Country People," seeing as you're happy about good country people throwing out their empty PBR cans. You can't use that title, either. So settle on something like "Captain of the Solitaire Team," because you've been thinking about how all these home-schooled kids living in the area don't have sports teams or after-school activities.

Okay. Now go out, walk a good mile and a quarter down the two-lane road, and get your fifty cans. Bring them home, stomp on them, and add them to the rest.

DAY SIX

Reread the finished story. Make some changes. Print out a few copies. Go out and get another fifty cans, which might take you a mile and a half of walking. When you get home, stand on the scale and notice that all this walking has caused you to lose almost four ounces of weight. Maybe you shouldn't have been eating all those Little Debbie Oatmeal Creme Pies while you wrote.

Now gather your cans and take them down to a place that buys scrap metal. Turn in the cans. On average, twenty-five cans weighs about a pound. You'll turn in ten pounds of aluminum cans — which will come to about $5 on today's market. Use that money to buy stamps. Buy six first-class stamps, and as many subsequent-ounce stamps as possible. I realize postal rates will go up in the future. But then again, maybe the price of recyclable aluminum will skyrocket.

Always be optimistic, like I am.

A 5,000 word story usually runs about

eighteen pages. Every four pages of typing paper weighs an ounce. Your story, plus the cover letter—which will only read "Dear Editors, Please consider the enclosed story, 'Captain of the Solitaire Team,' for an upcoming issue."—will cost less than a buck-fifty to mail. And you'll need a regular business-sized SASE enclosed for response. So that costs, say, a few bucks, tops. You'll almost be able to send your story out to three places, which, for some reason, is frowned upon by some editors, but what the hell—you wouldn't apply for one job at a time, would you? And the editors are way up in New York, more than likely, and so won't send down their unpaid interns to rough you up because the unpaid interns would stay for good, once they notice how you live in one of the cleanest square miles in America.

Maybe you should've picked up more than fifty cans a day, so you can send the story out more. I should've mentioned it's easy to find empty aluminum cans in the garbage bins at convenience stores, gas stations, in most parking lots, and so on. Maybe you understood that already. I hope so. I'm hopeful you got obsessed about picking up aluminum, and that you have enough extra stamps. I know it happened to me. When people ask me—rudely, I think—about my retirement plans, I say I have all my money wrapped up in the aluminum market.

Now send out your story to *The New Yorker, Harper's, The Atlantic Monthly, Playboy, Esquire,* or any of those slick magazines that pay upwards of $3,000 a story. The chances of two of those magazines wanting the same story are slim.

Don't sweat over it. If you do sweat over it, just think of it as another way to lose weight.

Wait! Maybe you haven't been paying attention to the ways of the internet world! It seems that a slew of places—well, almost all of them—make you submit work online. No more stamps, but it still costs, usually, three bucks through this thing called *Submittable*. So shove your aluminum can money into a PayPal account, et cetera. Thank all the gods for not having to lick stamps.

DAY SEVEN

Start over. Start a new story. Write 1,000 words. Go out and pick up cans, and notice how you're now walking farther. Or further. Make a note to get out the dictionary and look up the difference between those two words when you get home, stomp, and wash your hands. Do the same for *lay* and *lie* so you no longer have to write sentences like, "I reclined on the couch" or "You're telling a big fat untruth!"

DAY EIGHT

Don't be discouraged by the rejection from *The Atlantic Monthly*. It'll appear that the fiction editor rented a Learjet to give you the bad news. How did the post office get the manuscript to him, and he get the answer back so quickly? you'll wonder. He's that fast.

Rewrite the first 1,000 words of the second story, write another 1,000, and realize you need to get the first story back out in the mail soon. You might have to jack up the number of cans per day, for you'll need more postage.

END OF YEAR TWO

You finally hear about that first story you sent off from those magazines that weren't *The Atlantic Monthly*. Because you've sent a story a week to them you think, *Man, they're still holding 103 stories of mine.*

Meanwhile, you've taken each story and sent it off to literary journals that pay fifty bucks a page, or twenty-five, or ten. You've started sending to places that'll offer you contributor's copies.

But that's all right. You're up to walking anywhere from six to ten miles a day in order to find fifty cans. You've lost twenty pounds or more.

YEAR EIGHT

The Atlantic Monthly takes a story. Or *Harper's*. No matter what or where, you get three to five thousand dollars upon signing the contract.

Do not go out on a fifteen-year drinking binge. Promise me that you'll not go on a fifteen year drinking binge.

Take the money and invest it in either a CD getting questionable interest, or in a mutual fund that's not Putnam Voyager B.

YEARS NINE THROUGH FIFTEEN

You've sold enough stories now to a few of the slick magazines, you've told a number of agents you were "thinking about" writing a novel, you've been anthologized, and you've been in a number of literary magazines.

You still live in a trailer, but the countryside is spectacular.

You've invested all that money and can now

boast about being a twenty-thousand-dollaraire.

YEARS SIXTEEN THROUGH TWENTY

Surely someone will take a chance on publishing your first collection of stories. You've now written 832 of the things, ten of which are okay.

You look good, except for all those nasty sores and lesions on your hands from forgetting to properly wash them after getting cut by aluminum cans.

YEAR TWENTY

Sign the book deal, no matter what. Like the rest of your money, stash 90 percent of the picayune advance into a CD or mutual fund that's not Putnam Voyage B. Take what's left over to wash and wax your trailer.

AFTER TWENTY YEARS

You'll never understand the workings of interest rates, but over time—notice how you don't have kids with which to bother, or a spouse, seeing as you've slightly focused on your work—your savings will grow and grow and grow. You'll get more book deals, and a chance to leave the trailer in order to speak to people at colleges. They'll pay you more than the magazines, somehow. And you'll speak at writers conferences, even though you never attended one over all those years.

You never attended because (1) they cost way too much money; and (2) you rightly *wrote* over that time instead of *talking* about writing.

CAVEATS

This little outline, of course, must be adjusted if you have a full-time job on the side. Maybe you have medical problems that need to be looked into. Maybe you live in a dry county where there's not enough discarded beer cans. Maybe you live in a county with a high rate of diabetes, and there aren't Coke or Pepsi products laying or lying around. Maybe it's difficult to write a story a week—one every month is fine, but you'll have to multiply all those years up above by four. Maybe the trailer gets hit by a tornado, and you lose the will to live. Maybe you went on that fifteen-year binge like I've heard most writers do. Maybe you fell in love with someone coming from the other direction, picking up cans off the side of the road, and now there's a bad jealous rivalry going on between two writers.

Well, then, don't write.

THE DAILY GRIND

ON OCCASION, I walk into one of the local coffee shops near where I work. There's a Starbucks, of course, but then there are others that may or may not be part of a chain: Port City Java, Coffee Underground, Coffee Beanery, Joel's Java, You're the Juan, Jitters, Shaky's, The Burro's Back, Postcards from Tijuana. There are sharecroppers working larger land tracts in the South than the square quarter-mile where these roasting businesses seem to thrive. Usually I have to wade in, look at the glaze-eyed teenager working the counter, and say, "Just give me a regular Regular. House blend. A regular old regular coffee, close as you can get to Folgers or Maxwell House or Yuban or Chock Full o'Nuts."

In the past, the counter people usually cocked their heads to one side, and for a while I thought they'd never heard of these brands. Maybe they thought, What kind of coffee doesn't have the word *forest, jungle, pampas,* or *biodiversity* in its title? Then I realized that they couldn't hear me — all the noise — not only the mournful, suicide-inducing music playing overhead, but the constant tapping of fingers on keyboards.

This has to stop immediately.

Let me say now I have never walked into,

say, Daily Grind and found athletes scattered around the tables, performing squat thrusts, doing crunches and push-ups, or counting out sets of curls. Nor have I seen seamstresses roll out bolts of cloth, cut out patterns, then whip out their sewing machines. I've not seen veterinarians haul in their sick canines, pull them out of portable pet carriers, and administer rabies and Parvo vaccinations. There have been exactly zero potters working their wheels, taxidermists stuffing their bobcats, toxicologists using petri dishes to play checkers, circus performers practicing their knife throwing, pilots working some kind of virtual reality takeoff-and-landing apparatus, or exotic dancers using the sugar and cream kiosks as some kind of barre. One time I saw a general practitioner trying to drum up free breast exams, but he got kicked out.

So what's with all the so-called writers thinking their craft is some kind of spectator sport? When did novelists, essayists, poets—especially poets—come to the belief that everyone would be mesmerized, enchanted, and enthralled with having to look at their tortured selves staring blankly at the ceiling tiles before typing out something like "Her collection of Mardi Gras beads/like stringed coffee beans/remind me of the last time I saw her when she slapped me in the face and said, 'Get out, loser'"?

I don't get it. Knife throwers would be a different story, but not writers.

Now someone with a bigger heart and more patience might argue, "They're beginning writers, George. They can't afford the electricity to run their brand new laptops." Fine and dandy.

I don't notice them ordering regular Regular House Blend coffees the likes of Eight O'Clock, which cost, on average, $1.87 for a Grande, Venti, Enormé, Gordo, or whatever it's called. No, they're getting the things with chocolate syrup and whipped cream and sprinkles, which cost upwards of six bucks. I'm no mathematician, but six times thirty comes to $180. No one pays $180 a month to provide electricity for a hovel — where beginning poets should live, by the way.

"They need to view the outside world for ideas, George. Writers — young and old — need to experience life around them."

Okay, this argument almost makes sense. Great. I've already pointed out that there are no veterinarians, seamstresses, taxidermists, toxicologists, exotic dancers, or knife throwers inside these places. So what's to write about? People ordering cups of coffee? Other miserable poets? If these coffeehouse denizens want to see the world and write about it, then they should pack up their laptops and Moleskins, jump a freight train to somewhere like North Dakota or Patagonia, and drink campfire coffee with hobos and gauchos.

I ask that everyone out there who walks into a coffee shop, sees someone wearing an ascot, smoking an imaginary pipe, fiddling with eighteen metal rings stapled into his or her face, and straining to come up with a synonym for "desperate," please go up to said "writer" and say, "What do you think about Faulkner? How's about the good old Agrarian poets? Hey, let's you and me recite some of James Dickey's poems together."

If you're lucky the beanhead will ask, "Who are these magical writers of which you mention?" Then you can point out how those writers all had small rooms off at the far end of their houses, with maybe some framed pictures of their dogs, dead dogs, and spouses on their desks, near their typewriters. There were half-filled bottles, more than likely, and empty ones that brought luck at one time or another. There were ashtrays, knives, smooth stones, found pennies, and bones of one sort or another there, too. Fishing lures. A list of editors who've either shown interest, or wrongly misread the writer. Some voodoo dolls. Packs of matches, folk art, and a dictionary. This is how a writer's workplace should appear. Never shall the words sprinkles or whipped cream show up.

If the would-be writer looks befuddled, then you can point out the nearest public library, a place where more writers should hang out if indeed they don't own a desk. In order to clean up America best, keep a list of all the public libraries from North Dakota to Chile.

WHERE I DISCOVERED
NARRATIVE POSSIBILITIES,
POSSIBLY

I BECAME A fiction writer, I'm convinced, because of barbecue. Back in 1975 and 1976, when I was a junior and senior at Greenwood High School in South Carolina, a few friends of mine and I would pile into my car and leave the parking lot surreptitiously at 11:55 a.m. in order to drive 2.5 miles to Little Pigs Barbecue, eat quickly, and drive back in order to attend our 12:30 English class. This took planning and guile, of course. First off, students weren't allowed to leave campus at lunch. I don't recall for certain, but I think one received four demerits for leaving campus without a certified note. At ten demerits one received a three-day suspension. So it took our walking right out of the building, acting like we knew what we were doing, then driving off when the assistant principal wasn't on patrol.

Also, it took knowing the owner of Little Pigs Barbecue, my friend Brother's momma, Ms. Scott. She had our orders ready when we arrived. The pitmaster of sorts—he tended the smoker out back— always smiled at us when we scrambled in, and he said something relatively unintelligible like "Boys messin', comin' here, school, waitin' for y'all, been stokin' fire, ha!"

145

It wasn't unlike dealing with James Brown at a picnic. One of the pitmaster's legs was shorter than the other, and he had scar-burned arms as lean and tense as steel cables. People called him Slim, or Smoky, as I recall.

Listen, if any part of the plan backfired, I had a slew of excuses available, the first of which being that my dentist, Dr. McBride, had his office right next door to Little Pigs, and that I'd handed over my note to the woman at the front office — she must've lost it — and that I was getting my teeth cleaned after eating, et cetera. Or — I had a track meet later in the afternoon and I always ran best with a belly full of pulled pork sandwiches topped with cole slaw, drenched in the hot variety of tomato-based sauce. Or — Sir, I graduated last year.

I came up with all kinds of lies, and fortunately never had to use any of them.

At the time, I didn't know I wanted to write fiction, though I'd started reading like all get-out, trying to catch up on what I felt like a seventeen- or eighteen-year-old kid was supposed to know before college. There wasn't a bookstore in my hometown — a Waldenbooks opened while I was in college, then closed — and I didn't really have a mentor who could tell me to read anything other than those godawful classics that start with "Wuthering" and end in "Heights." Something about barbecue, though, fueled my imagination. I had choices to make: hot, mild, or sweet sauce, how much to order, cole slaw on the bun or on the side? Did I want sliced or pulled pork? What about a combo plate?

The patrons, too, got me to thinking — What

other places in South Carolina catered to mill hands, lawyers, men, women, Blacks, Whites, and runaway high school students simultaneously? Barbecue, as they say, may have been the great equalizer of my training grounds—crippling choices, strange dialects, and the constant fear of getting caught doing something wrong.

Nothing but inspiration can emanate from this particular recipe.

In 2011 I drove 3.1 miles down the 72 By-Pass in my ex-hometown. I spoke into a Clear Voice Plus Microcassette-corder and listed off the fast food chains I saw on both sides of the road. McDonalds, Burger King, Hardee's, Dairy Queen, Sonic, Chick-fil-A, Zaxby's, Pizza Inn, Pizza Hut, Papa John's, Little Caesar's, KFC, Bojangles, Cap'n D's, et cetera. Outback, Chili's, Ruby Tuesday, Applebees, Moe's Southwestern. Subway, another McDonald's, Firehouse Subs, Taco Bell, another Bojangles, Ryan's, Red Lobster, IHOP, and so on. Huddle House, Waffle House, Cracker Barrel, Shoney's. There were forty-two of these places over the distance of a 5K run. That's an average of one per just over a hundred yards. I don't want to pick on my ex-hometown—I'm sure it's this way in other places—but what happened to the locally-owned restaurants, places where the cooks and/or chefs used some imagination, so that the patrons could incorporate some imagination in their own choices?

"Uhhhhh, I'll have a cheeseburger," or "Uhhhhh, I'll have a piece of pepperoni," or "Uhhhh, I'll have the cold cut on white bread," isn't going to foster any kind of future creativity from ne'er-do-well truants, if you ask me.

The Hash House closed down. The Try Me Restaurant, where I ate fried chicken back in the summers of my college days while working as a garbage truck driver, closed, also. I backtracked down the 72 By-Pass to Montague Avenue, then took a left toward town. Little Pigs Barbecue had changed hands, but it's still open. The outside smoker's been replaced with an indoor contraption, but at least pre-pattied frozen barbecue's not being shuttled in via one of those wholesale food suppliers.

"Wha'chew need, honey?" the woman asked me as I stood beneath the Order Here sign.

Oh, man, I had some flashbacks. My buddy Brother Scott now goes by his given name, Jesse, and is a history professor. I have no real clue as to my old friends' whereabouts—Charlie, Jeff, Brillo—who piled into the car, though I could see them all, elbows on the table, barbecue sauce draining from wrists to elbows.

I didn't tell this new woman anything about plot and character, that I needed some new ideas, that I might be sitting at a table a little longer than the rest of the patrons—who looked about the same as when I snuck in here back before the world fell apart.

A FINE RESTAURANT IN NOWHERE, SOUTH CAROLINA, RUN BY A MAN NAMED XUE

E VERY YEAR, I think it is necessary, for some reason, to grow a lot of jalapeños, habaneros, and cayennes. Because I'm 151 years old, I am not able to eat these fruits anymore without unspeakable repercussions. One day last summer, I had already frozen two gallons of jalapeños. I'd eaten about another quart, and paid the price. So this year, when the habaneros came in, I thought, What will I do with these things? My father taught me long ago that there were children in other countries without peppers that registered 300,000 on the Scoville Heat Scale.

Because any restaurant around here that ventures away from the meat-and-three motif practically makes the news, I was aware of a relatively new sushi and hibachi restaurant on Highway 123 in Easley, South Carolina—halfway between Greenville and Clemson—called Dozo. I had heard the place had near-sublime experimental cuisine. So I showed up unannounced, as is my wont, toting along a freezer bag filled with my peppers. "Hey," I said to the sushi chef. This was lunchtime. The place was packed. "Y'all want any peppers? I mean, I grew all these peppers and I can't use them. You can have them for nothing."

Xue Yang, the chef, looked at the bag and, in better English than I'll ever speak, said, "Oh, man, yeah. The guys in back will find something to do with them."

I later learned that Xue Yang's father and mother were Laotian Hmong farmers. During the Vietnam War, they escaped to Thailand, and then, in 1980, to Minnesota (with Xue in the womb), where thousands of Hmong became relocated to escape genocide. Minnesota, as it ended up, wasn't quite the place for a Southeast Asian farmer to continue what he knew best. So the Yangs moved to Fresno. They had eight children, and later had Chia, who soon thereafter asked to be called "Sean," because his given name reminded Americans of that damn clay animal figurine with the sprouts growing out of its body in late-night TV infomercials of the 1980s.

Mr. Yang grew cherry tomatoes in Fresno. Little Xue and Sean took kung-fu lessons. Sean showed a particular expertise, beating grown men in tournaments. Meanwhile, Fresno's Hmong population grew, and gangs thrived. In order to keep them out of trouble, Mr. and Mrs. Yang sent their sons off to live with relatives in Wisconsin, then brought them back home, back and forth, and so on.

When he was in high school, Xue Yang took a job at a Chinese restaurant in Fresno. He worked as a busboy, as a dishwasher, as kitchen help. Soon thereafter, he worked at a more famous restaurant, one that got written up in the local papers. He learned how to work the hibachi.

Then, an older Yang brother moved to Mooresville, North Carolina. He had a friend who opened up a restaurant two hours away. The new restauranteur had no knowledgeable people in the kitchen, so this friend asked Xue's brother to make a call back to California, and Xue left the West Coast. He was twenty years old. "They took me in. They set me up with a place to live. They treated me as family," Xue says.

They told him to do what he wanted. "On Mondays, I did sushi," Xue explains. "Tuesdays, I waited tables. On Thursdays, I washed dishes. I did everything, from managing to busing tables and washing dishes. Then they sold the restaurant."

Xue had spent six and a half years there.

Xue Yang thought about moving back to California, but in a matter of a week he found three jobs. One job was in my hometown of Greenwood, South Carolina, oddly enough. Another was at a sushi place nearby that's no longer in business. A Chinese man named "Jimmy" hired him on—I pointed out how his name probably wasn't really "Jimmy," and Xue stared at me like I'd lost my mind. Jimmy had four chefs in the back, a manager, two more kitchen helpers, and six or seven servers. Anyone with a sense of mathematics knows that he had too many people on the payroll.

Then the economy tanked. Xue called up his brother Sean, who was working hibachi restaurants in Atlanta. "In the Atlanta market—

inner Atlanta—there are about a hundred hibachi restaurants," Sean says. "Outer Atlanta has about another two hundred. It's a hibachi chef's dream."

Sean's experience emanated from the Fresno restaurants, also. In Atlanta, he performed from ten in the morning until ten at night, working the hibachi, six days a week, for a year. He learned the food, experimented with spices, mixed and matched by trial and error. Sean went from a smaller restaurant to the chains, and realized he would never get a raise. I guess after a hibachi chef learns how to juggle every available menu item, a certain sense of chef ennui develops.

"I called up Sean and I said, 'Dude, I'm going to open a restaurant. I found a location. The guy wants out," Xue says.

They took over the joint, renaming it "Dozo" (which, by the way, means "please"). I showed up with my bag of peppers. I've been eating either lunch or supper there, more or less, four or five times a week, whether or not they like me showing up.

Xue Yang is now thirty, his brother Sean, twenty-nine. Xue is married to Jin, a lovely Chinese woman who has a master's degree from Clemson University. She does the books, figures out the computer, and greets the customers in a friendly way that brings to mind someone whom St. Peter would hire to bring nervous sinners into the Pearly Gates. Sean does hibachi, along with a Vietnamese chef named Cong who likes to bow-hunt in his spare time and wears a John

Deere toque he stitched up himself. Lin Lan Juan — and I have never understood this last name/first name stuff that goes on in Chinese culture — goes by "Wendy," and she works the tables, along with Brett and some others. Wendy told me that, to make my wife happy, I needed to boil her an egg on her birthday. Easy enough. I like Wendy, or Lin, or Lan Juan. Sean got her one of those Rosetta Stone bombardment tutorials for her birthday. I don't know for sure, but I think it comes with workbooks, CDs, maybe even a hologram of a tutor speaking in two languages. It has worked well — now Wendy can say "boil an egg on her birthday" without being self-conscious.

A few months after I brought the peppers and became a regular, Xue said to me, "We're going to celebrate Chinese New Year a few months early. You and Glenda come on by after we close up on Sunday night. I'm going to be making soup."

I usually hate soup. I said okay.

It wasn't regular soup. Three cauldrons of herbs were boiling, into which these ingredients landed: duck, chicken, clams, shrimp, lobster, congealed pork blood, lotus root, sea cucumbers, noodles, other noodles, weird noodles, things I couldn't identify as being flora or fauna, and so on. And, of course, it was the best concoction I've ever eaten.

"What the hell?" I asked. "What's going on here? Where did you get this idea?"

Later, there were loganberries, melons I'd never seen before, and some kind of grapefruit that looked like cotton candy on the inside.

"This is how Sean and I grew up," Xue says. "Our mother is a shaman. A lot of people in the community would come to her and say their daughter's sick or whatever. Could you perform a ceremony? Just say a lot of prayers and a blessing for her? Well, they sacrificed a pig or a cow, or something like that. They went to the slaughterhouse and they butchered the meat later. There's a dish they used to eat called laab—it's fresh meat, steak tartare. They season it with all these herbs."

"Cilantro. Basil. Parsley. Lemon. Lime," Sean says.

Xue continues, "A little bit of the juice of the gall bladder adds bitterness to it, and you eat it right away. It's delicious. We put these fold-out tables together. When it was dinner time, they brought the food out. Meats, veggies, seafood— all the way down. Everything was fresh. Nothing was store-bought. We didn't even know half the people there when we were kids. Our mother said, 'They are relatives.'"

Because I have been trained in making some kind of connections, however weak, seeing as I have a degree in philosophy, I say, "It's how you treat your customers. Like they're family."

Xue nods. He says, "Shamanism is all about ancestors. We have their pictures on the wall."

According to Xue, here are the types of people who show up at Dozo: nurses, teachers, parents with their kids (to the hibachi section), HVAC repairmen, people who work for DHEC, me, doctors, lawyers, pharmacists, my banker, pastors, sorority women from Clemson, high school coaches, librarians, my mechanic, my neighbor the hand surgeon, my neighbor the electrician, and about everyone in between. For the most part, Xue says, people who sit in the sushi section of Dozo are open-minded. "I've never met anyone on the sushi side who wasn't intelligent. If I say to them, 'You might want to try the monkfish liver,' they say 'Okay, I'll try it.'"

"The ones who come to the hibachi side want filets, rare, medium rare, and the lobsters, and a show for the kids," says Sean.

"Sean's more theatrical. He likes performing. He won all those trophies back when we had kung-fu competitions," Xue says.

"Man, they're paying to see a show and eat good food," Sean says. "Meanwhile, I'm trying to get them to venture out and eat, say, the Godzilla Roll" — ordered from the sushi side of the restaurant.

Mmmmmmm, the Godzilla Roll: tuna, yellowtail, salmon, and kani (crab) in tempura with eel sauce, spicy mayo, scallion, and masago (roe).

In the aforementioned list of People Who Eat at Dozo in Nowhere Easley, South Carolina — where I implore people to show up, so it doesn't go out of business, because I'm so goddamn selfish and do not want to have twelve dozen meat-and-three dives from which to choose — I should've included "Ex-Hollywood Film-Industry Person Now Retired Some Forty Miles Away" named Richard. Who knows why Richard moved from California to one of the

Cliffs at Keowee upstate South Carolina resorts? He's in his seventies. Maybe he wanted to film a documentary on our governor — I don't know. Maybe he liked the inexpensive greens fees at golf courses. I just know that I sit by him at lunch, and he, like me, has selfish ways. He's eaten sushi in New York, California, Seattle, Japan, and elsewhere. He says he's never eaten sushi as fresh and as good as at Dozo.

"Richard came in the first time," Xue says, "and he looked at my sushi bar. He ordered one item at a time. He was very picky. He looked at it, smelled it. He said, 'I'll try the hamachi (young yellowtail). Good. I'll try tako (octopus). Good.' He tried every piece, piece by piece. Well, we got through the routine of his coming in once or twice a week, and then he reached into his wallet and pulled out a piece of paper that he carried around with him. I said, 'What's this?' And he said, 'When I lived in L.A., I ate sushi every day, so I wrote down what I liked so I wouldn't forget.'

"I looked at it. It was all in Japanese. I recognized one or two of the items. Later, I called my vendor and he said, 'Yeah, I got these. Like sea cucumber, and marinated sea-cucumber intestines, bonito intestines, and mountain yams.' So I got it for him. What went over well, I kept on the menu. Fatty tuna. Spicy cod eggs. He likes pickled burdock roots. Marinated gourd shavings. Radish sprouts. Dry cod."

On a side note: I think it would be a great idea to have a hot dog, slathered in mustard and onions, rolled in rice, and cut into pieces for some kind of Tailgate Roll. Or Vienna sausages, in a Redneck Roll. Xue defers.

If you ask me, it all comes back to family. On the menu board, apart from the hand-out menu, one will find the Will, Gwen, Tommy, or Bob Roll—combinations that regulars have suggested. One time I went into Dozo and Xue said, "Hey, George, do you like oysters?" I said, "Uh-huh," and he said, "Try this"—an oyster covered in cheese, crab, spicy mayo, and roe. "What do I owe you?" I said.

"Man, I'm trying it out, brother, trying it out," he said. The same went for the whole squid cut up like onion rings with eel sauce, and the fatty tuna, and the giant live clam boiling at the bottom of the bowl amidst other seafoods. "You have to keep going. When you stop and think you're already the best, that nobody can beat you, that's when you go under. We're ready to change and grow all the time."

I should mention that no matter what one orders, one receives a jelly-fish/octopus/ seaweed salad gratis. I should mention that one time I was in Dozo and a drifter of sorts came in and sat down. Xue made him said salad, and sent it over via Lin Lan Juan, or Lan Juan Lin, or Wendy, or whatever her name is, the guy ate it, and then he left without paying. Xue said to me, "He looked hungry." He said, "He looked like one of my uncles." I should mention that after the doors close every night, the staff holds some kind of cook-off, wherein employees use anything available, e.g., those peppers I brought in on Day One. I think it was at one of these cook-offs where Sean came up with the "Electric Eel Roll," which was really cream cheese and crab, plus a handful of scattered Pop Rocks, which made the thing sizzle. Nice practical joke. Not something that ended up on the menu.

Anyway, I don't want to formally admit I think some kinds of socialism work. I won't say such a thing. Who needs happy, restaurant-working people living on this planet, trying to make other people happy?

FROM WRITING IN A ROOM THAT ONCE DISPLAYED JESUS, INSIDE A ZOO, INSIDE A BOTANICAL GARDEN

I'M SUPERSTITIOUS, for one, and perhaps an as-of-yet diagnosee of Attention Deficit Disorder. When I'm working, I need to face, at worst, a bookcase, and at best a blank wall. If there's a window in front of my desk, I'll watch for squirrels and birds, bad weather, the neighbors playing corn hole. I'll count leaves on a tulip poplar, and pray a snake crawls up, et cetera. I seemed to have barged in on a few families of possums who make themselves at home on the deck, beneath my Jeep, in the trees. There's a wake of black buzzards on the closest cell tower, maybe a hundred yards away, then a hundred yards up in the air. More often than not, at dawn I look up and see more than a few of them perched, staring down at me, their wings splayed out like odd Phoenixes.

So the previous owners—a nice couple who install big-time kitchens, thus what sold the house to Glenda, seeing as these folks put in a couple gas Wolf stoves and a hood normally seen at a Waffle House—maybe had been color-blind. Downstairs, the rooms were painted a yellow brighter than goldfinches. Then there was the lime green living

159

room. The laundry room was a shade of orange not known to sane people, the bedroom some kind of blue. If one took off the roof and looked down, it wouldn't have looked that much different than four or five tubs of sherbet, or a bag of saltwater taffy. Maybe the previous owners had gone to the Caribbean on a second honeymoon and became enthralled with the color schemes of local bodegas. Upstairs, one of the rooms had that wallpaper that looked like rows of books. It's not like I don't have books. Why would I need bookshelf wallpaper behind actual bookshelves filled with books?

But there's the best room, and it's where I write now: They had hired out some local muralists to transform a perfectly normal room — probably once used as a child's bedroom or office. Four normal walls became a jungle, the ceiling a sky with a bald eagle flying across. On the day after closing I drove over to the new house, armed with whatever paint colors Lowe's or Home Depot make up. Me, I call these paints "dark green" and "white," but they have special names. I got out a roller and eradicated the eagle, and felt a little unpatriotic doing so. Then I got to the walls and erased the lemurs and rhinos, the elephants and gorillas. I thought to myself, how in the world would I have ever been able to write up here with all these animals' eyes looking down on me? I painted over giraffes, a sloth, tigers, lions, chimpanzees, spider monkeys, antelope, egrets, snapping turtles, penguins. Lots of green and yellow flora worked as a border of sorts, down near the baseboard.

A dachshund showed up. Okay, so at this

point I'd already thought, how is a penguin going to survive in the jungle, and I wasn't sure if tigers and lemurs shared the same habitat.

But the wiener dog made me stop. Maybe they had a wiener dog and wanted him memorialized in this odd cosmos.

And then I came across Noah's ark, crashed into a snow-covered mountaintop.

Farther down, Jesus on the cross.

Oh, man. I'm not the most religious person in the world, but like I started off, I do own a number of superstitions. I meant to block off the Jesus part of the mural and leave it — He would be covered with a bookcase — but maybe the paint fumes got to me and I lost my concentration. I rolled right over Jesus, not even thinking. I thought, *That can't be a good thing to do,* and then wondered if it might later cause me to sit here at the computer, not write as much as I used to write, then — out of superstition — presently move my desk in front of the window and get tempted by all the flora and fauna outside, calling for me to come look at them as if I were some kind of nature writer.

Wait — a stink bug just crashed into my head. There are stink bugs all over the place. Nubby the cat just said to me, "Don't forget the stink bugs," seeing as they make his entire life worth living. "Don't mess with me" — Nubby can speak in English somehow.

So that's about it. Oh, on occasion it sounds as if a ball bounces down the staircase. More than a few times Glenda says she's left the bedroom, then come back to find one of the Venetian blinds closed when both had been open. The

TV changes channels on its own at times. We've heard crashes, looked at each other, then gone to find nothing displaced.

But maybe it's Jesus trying to creep through the paint, you know—how hard could that be? Is it those buzzards trying to crash-land into the house knowing that there's something dead inside the walls? Do the stink bugs have more kamikaze power than I've given them credit?

I blame it on the possums, roaming around with their bad selves, eating ticks so I don't have to deal with another scourge.

Aside: I didn't mean to do so, but after I'd tamped the lids back on the paint, taken up the drop cloth, and admired my job, I noticed that I'd left a three-by-three foot section of flora beneath a window that is now behind my desk. I could've easily fixed the problem. But I'm lazy.

Another aside: My father told me, more than once, and starting at about age twelve, that if one learned to paint houses, one will never be out of a job. True.

WHY I WRITE FIRST DRAFTS BY HAND

MAYBE I WOULD'VE published my first book before forty-two had someone not stolen my beautiful, metallic-blue Smith Corona electric typewriter at some point between one and eight in the morning in Greenville, South Carolina. Until that point I'd been rolling paper in the carriage, typing out first drafts, and, understanding them to be done, sending the manuscripts off to editors. I had a lot to learn. I was twenty-two years old and one month out of school, with a degree in philosophy, which is to say I was working at a Budweiser warehouse. My "apartment," for lack of a better word, cost $180 a month. What little of it there was had a nine-foot ceiling and those hip old steam radiators I would've used had I made it to winter. This was mid-July and the place didn't have air conditioning, so I kept a box fan in the window and it made such a racket that my sleep went undisturbed as the thief jimmied my door open and walked off with my TV, stereo, pocket watch, and the typewriter.

When I woke up and saw my front door wide open, I thought to myself, standing there naked, Wow, I forgot to close the door last night.

And then I put it together that I was no longer the proud owner of "belongings." At the time, I cared most about my TV and stereo, about watching the Atlanta Braves on the old WTBS and cranking The Clash, Tom Waits, Richard Hell and the Voidoids. The watch was a gold-plated number with a hunter on one side and a fisherman on the other that my father had bought me ten years earlier, maybe in hopes I'd become one with nature. I went into the kitchen and felt some relief that the burglar hadn't taken my one pan, and the glasses I'd procured from another part-time job washing dishes at Steak and Ale.

I thought I deserved it. Like I said, I was twenty-two and worked at a Budweiser warehouse. I'd stolen beer and thought doing so had beckoned bad ju-ju/voodoo/karma. Somehow Greenville had been tabbed as a test market for selling longneck bottles in regular stores. My job was to take longneck bottles out of a regular box, place them in six-pack cardboard carriers, then shove the six-packs back into the original box. These went onto a pallet, and another seasonal guy named Bobby drove a forklift to take loaded pallets to a truck. Maybe twice a week, when no one was looking, I carried a case to the trunk of my 1974 Toyota Corolla, telling my boss later, "Fucked up and dropped another case." He never questioned me. I had no shortage of friends then, showing up at parties as I did fully cumbered.

Then I noticed the typewriter gone from its perch on an ancient oaken desk salvaged from a defunct, pre-integration high school. I thought it might be a sign I should never write again. The gods had come down and made the decision—"C'mon, George, you're too stupid to write." I'd started writing fiction, after all, because I was sick of friends making fun of my poetry and one-act plays. A woman named Jessica Einstein that I studied abroad with once said, not that unrightly, to me, "You're just going to end up being one of those bitter unpublished writers." It was easy for me to believe her then. Writing would end up killing me, would turn me into a hermit and misanthrope. I was meant to work in the warehouse and steal beer until caught. Maybe take the LSAT, become a lawyer, do what I could to make the world a worse place.

Wanting to look for the guy, I threw on some clothes and went to grab my car keys. My keys! They were gone, too. To take a man's TV, stereo, watch, and typewriter is one thing, but to steal his car is another thing altogether, almost anti-American.

When I reached the parking lot, I saw the driver's side door open. I found the keys in the ignition. Luckily, the one engineering marvel on a 1974 Toyota Corolla is that the seat belt has to be engaged for the engine to turn over. I imagined the thief or thieves loading up the back seat, then turning the ignition and assuming the battery was dead. "Why does nothing work out easily?"

God. I knew the feeling. I was infected with the writing disease. During my senior year in college I'd started a novel that ended up as 450 pages of god-awful slap-stick. I took about a paragraph out of that manuscript and ended up with a 250-page novel of god-awful slapstick, lightly coated in pathos. I took about a sentence out of that manuscript and turned it into a 300-page manuscript of slapstick, pathos, irony, and satire. And I wrote these 1,000 pages in Mead notebooks. Then I started writing short stories, finally. Even after I got another electric typewriter, the habit stuck.

Here's what I hope: I hope the son of a bitch who broke into my apartment pawned the TV and stereo and watch, but kept the Smith Corona. I hope he took it home and plugged it in and sat down thinking, "This can't be all that tough." I hope he then got a little taste of the rare pain one must endure to be a writer. That'd be punishment enough for me.

MY WRITING MENTOR

I DON'T KNOW how many of my friends and acquaintances, who are writers, say, "Well, I started reading William Faulkner at age twelve, and that's why I knew I would become a writer." Sometimes it's Shakespeare, or Thomas Wolfe. I believe my buddies, I guess, but I wonder where the hell they came across these writers. I grew up in a town without a bookstore, except for a place that advertised Books and Bibles, a place that seemed packed only with those yellow-and-black paperback Cliffs Notes for novels written by writers I'd be forced to read in high school: Charles Dickens, Upton Sinclair, Edith Wharton, the Brontës, Jane Austen, George Orwell, maybe George Eliot. I'm surprised there wasn't some kind of suicide problem back in the mid-Seventies, what with all these execrably depressing tales. I don't remember taking the SAT, but I suppose there were questions about these writers' works.

Me, I found myself attracted to a little man named Henry Gibson, who held a gigantic flower while spouting off "poems" on the television show *Laugh-In.* Henry Gibson later starred, occasionally, on *Murder, She Wrote,* a fine whodunit starring Angela Lansbury. He might've been involved—either as actor or director—in some other shows, I don't know. What matters to me is, he didn't ever have an entire chapter that went "My mother is a fish," like Faulkner did in *As I Lay Dying*. Gibson stared into the camera and recited poems that followed an AABB rhyme scheme, or, if he felt randy, an ABAB scheme. I loved the guy.

Aside: Back in 1974, I ran a ten-mile race at the inaugural Festival of Flowers festivity, in Greenwood, South Carolina. I'd hurt my big toe earlier in the month, and had to run with my right leg turned sideways somewhat. So I didn't have the best race. Some dude from Clinton, South Carolina, of all places, showed up. He'd been good enough to qualify for the 1972 Olympic Trials, and he ran the ten miles in something like 54 minutes. Me, limping, I came in first in my age group, but it wasn't my best race—something like 65 minutes. Give me a break. I was fifteen.

Another aside: Two years later I ran a half-marathon called the Paris Mountain Road Race. I sucked. I'd been in the best shape ever, and the Furman University coach had been courting me. As it ended up, I had the mumps. I ran the thing, though, in an hour and nineteen minutes.

Anyway, I plodded my way in on that ten-mile run at the Festival of Flowers race, which ended up on highway 254 there at Park Seed Company. My parents had a friend, named Tom Reynolds, an artist, who took care of Park Seed's catalogue.

Another aside: Tom Reynolds died of leukemia about two months after retiring. His wife, Carmen Reynolds, escaped Cuba back in the day.

So I finished the race, not knowing the inaugural Festival of Flowers' Grand Marshall was none other than Henry Gibson, and that he'd hand me a trophy for winning my Age Group, which happened to be 0-18.

So I got to college, thinking there was nothing comedic in writing, besides the non-published *Laugh-In* work of Henry Gibson. And somewhere along the line I came across Eugene Ionesco, Samuel Beckett, Thomas Pynchon, Donald Barthelme, John Irving, even Wittgenstein and Nietzsche. Hilarious! Two professors—Jim Edwards in philosophy and David Parsell in French—directed me toward a reading life that didn't send me toward killing myself.

So this is my nod toward people who understood not everyone needs to be immersed in, say, Dostoyevsky.

STRANGE LOVE IN A
SMALL PASTURE

IF YOU GO to one of those satellite images via computer and zoom in on the pasture at the corner of Thomas Mill Road and Hester Store Road — the fenced ten or so acres adjacent to a two-story stone house, across from the vacant two-story stone general store — in zip code 29640, you'll witness where this sad, relentless tale took place. This is Dacusville. Easy weepers beware. I don't usually think of myself as nostalgic, prone to cry, or melodramatic, but in September of 2010 I slowed down near this particular intersection, witnessed what occurred, pieced it together perfectly, and felt my heart wither more so.

Now, at times I've been known to be hyperbolic and, on good days, comedic. What I have to relate here is neither funny nor exaggerated. It involves a trailer fire, some bartered rabbits, a horse and pig that once lived apart; my good ex-auto mechanic Dean Nash, who lived a half-mile from me in the stone house and came down with MS in his mid- to late-thirties; and a deaf woman.

The old sway-backed mare was named Candy. The pot-bellied pig was named, unfortunately, Blackie. At one time Blackie lived with a family inside their trailer, across Thomas Mill Road from where Candy slowly grazed around in her pasture. The singlewide caught fire, the pig ran across the macadam, scooted beneath the split-rail fence, and, evidently, pig-trotted his way to the horse. A few days passed, as days do pass for burned-out trailer-dwelling people focused on retooling their lives, before Blackie's owners returned to the area to search for their pet.

There stood Blackie, portly and bottom-tusked as ever, beneath Candy the horse. "Come here, Blackie," the trailerless people called out, or something like that, according to Dean Nash, my ex-mechanic. These people walked forward toward their traumatized porcine trailermate.

Candy the horse whinnied hard and—maybe for the first time in years—reared up on her hind legs. She rotated her fetlock joints like one of those kung-fu masters warming up.

Dean had come out to witness this event, which paralleled some kind of Capulet/Montague scenario. The trailer people—now long gone from the area and uninterviewable—backed off. The man said, "Hey, do you want to buy a pig?"

"No," Dean said. "Well, I guess I can trade you something for it. You want some rabbits I raise?"

Dean used to build engines for NASCAR drivers. If I were prone to hyperbole in this particular essay I would write, at this point, how my Jeep could go 160 miles an hour because Dean Nash bored out whatever it is engine builders bore out. My old Jeep might hit 80. There seems to be a problem with the air conditioner, something my new good mechanic Johnny finds mysterious.

The man took the rabbits. Candy unreared herself. Blackie stood beneath her. By "beneath her" I mean "the pig mostly stayed directly beneath Candy's sagging belly," especially during rainstorms, for twelve years.

Now, whenever people came to my house for the first time, my directions went something like this: "Turn off White Horse Road and drive four miles. You'll cross the Saluda River. You'll see a life-size plastic bull in the front yard of some people with no landscaping tastes. At the intersection of 183 and Thomas Mill Road, take a right. Take the first left—you'll see a horse with a pig underneath it—onto Hester Store Road," et cetera.

Dean got diagnosed with multiple sclerosis in the late 1990s. It got to where he couldn't climb the stairs in his house, and he put it up for sale. He folded up his mechanic shop out back and sold the house, the shop, his land, and Candy and Blackie. Part of the deal involved the new owners taking care of the horse and pig.

So for a dozen-plus years nothing changed when I gave people directions, at least up to the pig beneath the horse part. I should mention that, over the years, a new church sprouted up in a Butler building next to the pasture, a whole trailer park showed up behind where Blackie's first owners' trailer burned down, a field behind the old stone Hester Store got developed into a number of 5-10 acre tracts, and so on. A Clock's Original Drive-In opened, and a Spinx gas station. There's a Christian Ladies workout place that opened and closed, and a chiropractor's office, and a sun-tanning place.

So then it happened that I drove home at dusk and saw Candy on her side, Blackie standing next to her. A veterinarian, Dr. Derek Wessinger, knelt at Candy's head. Her heart was giving out. "It was the most remarkable thing I've ever seen," he told me later. "That pig was talking to Candy, and laying against her. The pig was frantic, nudging her, pulling on her tail, then going over to pull on her mane. It was more than I could take, I tell you."

Candy had to be euthanized, finally. They placed a blue tarp over her body until she could be taken away. Blackie slept next to her. My better half, Glenda, called the next morning on her way to work, crying, and said, "That tarp blew away in the night. Blackie's right up against Candy's stomach."

My next-door neighbor, a pediatrician named Angie Millon, has horses and hires out Dr. Wessinger. He had told her he worried about Blackie, and a couple months after Candy's death Angie asked that I go see if maybe the pig's owners would let her adopt Blackie, so he could return to the equine world. I went over there—I'll talk to anyone about a horse and a pig, of course—but I'm not sure Blackie's owner understood me, for she's deaf. She did tear up as I talked about seeing Candy on the ground, so I guess she knew why I showed up unannounced at her abode.

Within a month or so, a black Labrador retriever and a Chihuahua—I'm not lying here—began palling around with Blackie in the pasture. At one point, I'm sure you could've looked on Google Earth, found an obese pig, a Lab wearing a red collar, and a dot, standing in a field, off the corner of Thomas Mill and Hester Store roads.

Listen, I've told this story to a number of people. They say it would make a great children's story, except for the trailer fire, the MS, and the death of a horse. Children, it appears, don't deserve the cruelties of love. And of course, it gets worse: I drove to work one day and came across a dead bobcat, ten feet off the road, nearly up to the fence where Blackie lived. I got out and nudged the thing—it was a beautiful specimen, and by the afternoon a traveling taxidermist had evidently happened by, for it disappeared—and thought to myself how I hadn't seen Blackie, or his new friends, in a while. Because I took Logic in college, it didn't take much to piece together what had more than likely occurred.

I have never gotten the courage to go ask the deaf woman whatever happened to her adopted pot-bellied pig. I can't take seeing people cry when good memories crop up over barnyard tragedies.

Unfortunately, I don't foresee these scenarios occurring much in South Carolina in particular, and the South in general, presently. We won't see Candy and Blackie living together. There will be a Starbucks in the pasture. No one will ever have to drive by, see the saddest friendship this side of *Animal Farm,* and cry. It will not be a better existence, in my opinion, for any of us.

As an aside, when I first moved to the area in 1992, a man drove a horse trailer filled with llamas up to some gas pumps at the local Texaco convenience store. I stood behind a man at the register wearing cutoffs, no shirt, and no shoes. He looked out the window for a long moment, turned to me, and said, "What the hell kind of donkeys is them?"

I've since moved to Spartanburg County. No matter. I still have my Dacusville.

ARISTOTLE AND
SOUTH CAROLINA

ARISTOTLE COULD NOT have written the *Nichomachean Ethics* in the state of South Carolina because that tome is all about moderation and South Carolina is a big old state of excess only. There is little notion of moderation. We have the beautiful Grand Strand, plus the bottom end of the Blue Ridge Mountains. But then we have that Savannah River Nuclear Site in Aiken County and the nearly-disastrous atomic bomb hole near Florence in Mars Bluff. We have the classic row houses of Charleston, plus more people living in trailers per capita than anywhere else in the United States. We have produced Strom Thurmond of the Dixiecrat era, and the forward-thinking Reverend Jesse Jackson. We have BMW, Michelin, and Sunoco—and we have cotton mills that have either burned down mysteriously or faded into skeletal remains to be renovated into outlandishly-priced condominiums. There is the "peachoid" water tower thing outside of Gaffney on I-85, and then the Abbeville Opera House. Just in case anyone thinks the opera house might be too beautiful for a small town, there is a place called Roughhouse Billiards a few doors down to even everything back out.

We have refurbished and renovated Greenville, but then there is Pedro's South of the Border down near Dillon. We pride ourselves on good, level-headed, brilliant, ex-governor Richard Riley — who later became the best U.S. Secretary of Education ever — and then we have Preston Smith Brooks who beat the hell out of Senator Charles Sumner with a cane because Sumner compared Brooks to Don Quixote. Who wants to be compared to Don Quixote?

There is the incomparable Eartha Kitt, who sang at least one song in French, and then later starred as Cat Woman on *Batman* — and then there is a man named Barney Odom who had a canine named Flat Nose the Tree-climbing Dog who probably showed up on *The Tonight Show* more often than Eartha Kitt.

We can brag about a number of students who score perfect SATs, and then shrink back embarrassed at the line of schools making up the Corridor of Shame up and down I-95.

There is the bizarre fire-eater and secessionist Laurence Keitt, who once attempted to choke a Pennsylvania congressman, and then David Drake, known as Dave the Slave, who was not supposed to know how to read and write but who put out clay pots and jugs pre-Civil War in Edgefield County that now sell for thousands upon thousands of dollars.

There's fire-hot Blenheim's Ginger Ale, and the Salley Chitlin Strut. We have the Trappist monastery Mepkin Abbey, and we have the Darlington International Speedway that is "Too Tough to Tame."

There's nothing in-between in these parts.

It is this notion of excess that gives all of our writers the daily conflicts that may arise when two or more excessive people, places, or ideas clash. You do not have to be the smartest person in the world as long as you are blessed to be plopped down between North Carolina and Georgia. You do not even have to sit down and invent stories of your own when you live in a place where strangers possessed with all kinds of odd notions are willing to tell their most personal secrets, quirks, habits, and scams.

So it should be no surprise that South Carolina has produced, encouraged, sponsored, and/or nurtured so many writers over the past few hundred years. Could James Dickey have written *Deliverance* without understanding the inherent excess of a primordial forest-turned-water-skiing Mecca? Could Dorothy Allison have written *Bastard Out of Carolina* without her upbringing? I doubt that Max Steele would have even considered his classic short story, "Ah Love! Ah Me!" without intuiting the unspoken-but-omnipresent class system of mid-twentieth century Greenville.

Would Pat Conroy have written his many great novels if his father had been stationed in Jacksonville or Camp Pendleton? Could Josephine Humphreys have written *Rich in Love* while living in, say, Delaware? Ron Rash's mill poems would never emanate from the state of Oregon, and his novels and short stories would never have germinated in Vermont. Padgett Powell's *Edisto* wouldn't be the same if titled *Monhegan*, or *Staten*, or *Maui*. Likewise, William

Price Fox's *Southern Fried* would never be a classic had he been living elsewhere and chosen *Nor'eastern Boiled.*

I daresay that all of the writers included within *The South Carolina Encyclopedia Guide to South Carolina Writers* owe their connections to the Palmetto State for the prose, poetry, and plays they have offered the world.

At times, I know, South Carolina—especially in the realm of politics—has been the brunt of jokes. The political landscape changes, evolves, diminishes, disappears. Fortunately, though, we can pride ourselves on past writers and look forward to the ones our state will forge out yearly.

THANKSGIVING

ONCE A WEEK, around 7:30 in the morning, I meet up with three other ex-professors over bagels and coffee, sometimes coffee and cinnamon buns if we've given up on diets. I'm the youngster in the group, at age sixty-four. The other three men are emeritus, aged 75, 70, and 69. I think they accept me because I'm the most liable to drive around and knock over mailboxes with a baseball bat in gated communities, then tell them about it with cream cheese covering half my upper lip.

We do not talk about the weather. We do not talk much about sports, wives, car engine repairs, house improvements, idiot colleagues of the past, obituaries, and anything else that might make us depressed or flustered. It's all how to save America, and the books we've been reading.

Two days ago, I looked across the table at the seventy-five year-old man—a guy who became an administrator after about thirty years of teaching foreign languages—and said, "Hey, tell me about that time you got hit by a car."

He should be writing this essay, by the way. I don't know if he's embarrassed about the story, or what. I'll change his name to Frank. It's a good strong name, and a wonderful adjective.

Frank has cycled across Europe, and up and down the East Coast. He stands about six-two, maybe weighs 180, and keeps his head shaved. He can talk eloquently about French wines, the World Cup, bad roofers, *Don Quixote,* whatever. Most of the time I sit there thinking, Please don't ask me a question. Ten years ago he hired me for some kind of fancy endowed chair thing to teach fiction workshops and Grit Lit. I've always been scared of him.

Frank said, "Well, I was riding on a two-lane road I'd ridden for twenty years. At a four-way stop, I stopped. I motioned to this woman 'Can I go first?' She waved her hand. A mile down the road I was going about eighteen miles an hour, looking at my peddles, when I saw, peripherally, the bumper of her car."

This accident happened in 2017. He'd just retired.

Somehow I didn't know the whole story — only that Frank got in an accident, but he'd be okay. He said, "When I woke up, the police and a fire truck were there. Evidently I got my left foot out of the peddle, but then skidded across the asphalt and banged my head into a cement curb. I wore my helmet, which saved me, I guess."

Of course I said, "Damn, man."

He said, "I was in ICU for a few days because they couldn't get my heart rate down."

No broken bones. Road rash everywhere. Memory problems.

Now, all of this story brought on flashbacks, ones I think about infrequently: When I was fourteen, in Greenwood, South Carolina, on highway 254, a woman hit me from behind at fifty-five miles an hour, while I rode my tragically-heavy Schwinn ten-speed. Luckily I had a friend in front of me. Evidently I flew off the bike, landed some feet up a telephone pole, and slid down. Man, I was out. I didn't regain consciousness for three days, and spent ten in Self Memorial Hospital.

This was near-dusk, and I had a flashlight attached to the handlebars.

The woman who hit me took off, but luckily the driver behind her caught the license plate. Or maybe it was the passenger, or one of the two women in the back seat—they all served food in the cafeteria of my junior high school, and came home from work late. These were women who'd scooped lima beans, or mashed potatoes, or kerneled corn on my segmented platter in the past. They'd handed over sloppy joes to me and smiled.

As it ended up, I didn't have any broken bones, but owned a couple blood clots. I still have a scar on my left upper ankle from the front sprockets of the bike. To this day I have smudge-like scars on my knees, elbows, and right upper hip.

Ten days in the hospital. Six weeks doing nothing until the blood clots dissolved or whatever. $2000 hospital bill (good god, can you believe this?) and a meeting with a judge, the woman who hit me in attendance, the judge saying she needed to pay my parents for the hospital bill, plus a new bicycle, which I got—a really nice Raleigh ten-speed I never rode, took to college four years later, and had stolen.

I don't remember ninth grade, if it matters.

I went, I took classes, and for some reason I did really well in French I but not much else. I remember, after I came out of a coma, that a nurse gave me an enema before I went in for a series of odd X-rays. I remember telling my mom, "They gave me an emnia, and I went to the bathroom in the bed!"

Here's an aside: Greenwood's a small town. They tried to get in touch with my parents. My neighbors knew that my parents went to the drive-in movie. I have no clue what my parents thought important to see without me. There, over the driver's side speakers, the guy in the concession stand announced, "Can the Singletons please come to the booth? There's an emergency." My father later told me that my mother became a Christian, praying from the Highway 25 Drive-In to the hospital.

Anyway, two months went past, I quit wearing pajamas over my abrasions for the entire summer, this girl named Jonie and another named Kim quit showing up to teach me how to French kiss on my parents' front porch, I went on with myself, and I took up distance running instead of riding a bike.

"After four months the doctor brought me in for cognitive tests," Frank said there at the coffee shop. "He had me count backwards from a hundred by sevens. He gave me that test they gave Trump, you know: Person, Woman, Man, Camera, TV."

We laughed. Then we went, "100, 93, uh, 86, um…"

Actually, of all people, I went, "100, 93, 86, 79, 72, 65, 58," quickly, and then stopped. I didn't want to show off, understand. But, in reality, I wanted to make sure I could kind of do it.

Frank said, "He told me I was fine, that I did well."

Two men behind us at the next table started talking about warehouse jobs they had in the peach industry, back when they just got out of high school. I turned around to find two guys, maybe older than I, who looked like lawyers. I thought it necessary to say, "My first job out of college? After I graduated with really meaningful degree in philosophy? Budweiser warehouse. What a mistake on Budweiser's part! I had to take twelve-ounce longnecks out of a box, place them in six-pack cardboard containers, then put them back in the box. Then I'd put them on a pallet so they could go to grocery stores. This was some kind of test-market thing, for Greenville. About every day I'd go, 'Oops, accidentally dropped a case,' but in reality I put a case in the trunk of my old Toyota."

One of the other guys with me—not Frank—whispered, "How can you do this, just talk to strangers?"

I said, "Damn, man, how can you learn anything without talking to strangers?" but secretly I wondered if, perhaps, this was a terrible repercussion from my previous head injury. I said, "Yeah. Maybe I shouldn't've barged in like that." I thought back out how comfortable I've always been when it came to including myself to anyone's conversation.

"Anyway," Frank said. "I got an offer to run a program over in Europe for a month. I'd done work for them in the past. This guy was leaving.

It was a lot of money, plus an apartment added. I said hell yes! I went for a month. And then for two months, and then for three. As it ended up, I was over there illegally, 'cause I didn't have a visa for that long. Well, my wife was there, and she went off to visit some people in Amsterdam, leaving me alone for a long weekend."

I zoned out a little. I envisioned that Schwinn bike, which got kept in my parents' crawlspace for years, the back wheel with its bumper-crater that looked like the letter C.

Frank said, "I don't know what happened. One night I woke up at three in the morning and I felt flooded with my entire life: my bad childhood, how I'd gone off to college, and then grad school, how I'd gotten a job teaching, then being an administrator — I thought, 'My life has been nothing. I've done nothing." That's all I obsessed about."

One of the other two guys said, "Goddamn, it's not true. You got a Ph.D. from Chapel Hill."

Frank shook his head. "I saw a radiator, and got up on it. I tried to open the window. I was going to jump out, but I couldn't get the window open enough."

No one said anything. We sat there for a solid minute. One of the men behind us said something about how they were growing oranges in Georgia now, that he'd seen a clip on CNN. Finally, I said, "I'm never going to ask you another question again."

Frank broke out in a smile, high-fived me, and said, "Fuck you, Singleton." He said, "I called my wife and told her about it, and she said, rightly, that we needed to get back to the

United States immediately."

A psychiatrist told my friend Frank—and I might have some of this wrong—that the frontal lobe, or something, holds all the past's memories. And that it keeps those memories locked up. The rest of the brain's working hard on little things, like Breathe, Here's How to Drive, Go Take a Shower, Walk, and so on. But sometimes that frontal lobe releases all the old memories, and it can be devastating. With a brain injury, such things can occur. That's what happened to Frank.

So here I sit, waiting. I'm writing this on Thanksgiving Day. Earlier, I peeled three pounds of sweet potatoes I grew and harvested this year. There's a chance it'll be my only memory, later on. I kind of hope that's the case.

§

PUBLICATIONS

Essays in this volume previously appeared in the following journals:

"Refuse" first appeared in *Don't Quit Your Day Job*, M P Publishing Limited.

"Seven Protective Popeyes" first appeared in *Howl*, Crown Publishers.

"Acting Squirrelly" first appeared in *Garden and Gun.*

"Back from the Grave" first appeared in *Garden and Gun.*

"Nu-Way Lounge and Restaurant" first appeared in *Garden and Gun.*

"Moon Pie" first appeared as "Down to the Graveyard," in *Oxford American.*

"Marking Territory" first appeared in *L-O-V-E Is a Four Letter Word*, Plume, a member of Penguin.

"Why We Don't Play Chess" first appeared in *Bark* magazine, and later in *Dog Is My Co-Pilot*, Three Rivers Press.

"An Ode to Hangover Cures" first appeared in *Oxford American.*

"How to Write Stories, Lose Weight, Clean up the Environment, and Make $1,000,000" first appeared in *Oxford American,* and later in *Pep Talks, Warnings, and Screeds,* Writers Digest Books.

"The Daily Grind" first appeared in *Oxford American,* and later in *Pep Talks, Warnings, and Screeds,* Writers Digest Books.

"A Fine Restaurant in Nowhere, South Carolina, Run by a Man Named Xue" first appeared in *Oxford American.*

"*from* Writing in a Room that Once Displayed Jesus, Inside a Zoo, Inside a Botanical Garden" first appeared in *Carolina Writers at Home,* Hub City Press.

"Why I Write First Drafts by Hand" first appeared in *Tin House.*

"Strange Love in a Small Pasture" first appeared in *State of the Heart,* University of South Carolina Press, 2015.

"Aristotle and South Carolina" originally appeared as "Preface," in *The South Carolina Encyclopedia Guide to South Carolina Writers,* 2014.

"Where I Discovered Narrative Possibilities, Possibly" first appeared in the Southern Foodways Alliance's *Gravy,* Issue 43.

"Thanksgiving" first appeared in *Cutleaf.*

§

ACKNOWLEDGEMENTS

This isn't even difficult or funny: Walter Robinson, Denton Loving, Keith Lesmeister, and Kelly March of EastOver Press, Beth Gilstrap for flawless copyediting, and all the other editors who asked for or agreed to these essays.

§

About the Author

PHOTO: Glenda Guion

GEORGE SINGLETON has published ten story collections, two novels, and one book of writing advice. His short stories have appeared in *Atlantic Monthly*, *Harper's*, *Playboy*, *Story*, *One Story*, *Zoetrope*, *The Georgia Review*, *The Pushcart Prize Anthology*, *New Stories from the South*, and elsewhere. His nonfiction has appeared in *Garden and Gun*, *Oxford American*, *Bark*, *Best American Food Writing*, and elsewhere. He's received a Guggenheim fellowship and is a member of the Fellowship of Southern Writers.

Until All You See is Sky
George Choundas

This award-winning author of short stories now turns to nonfiction, telling true stories with playful language and engaging wit. He sits in the lobby of the Boston Parker House Hotel at dawn to write and imagines what is going on in every head but his own; he survives in a new elementary school by means of *The Illiad;* he imagines the ends of all the near-strangers who populate our lives; and he wanders through Midtown Manhattan mapping the geography of its idiosyncratic but thoroughly intriguing denizens and visitors with the eye of an expert anthropologist of everyday life. These are the best sort of essays— full of unforgettable characters rendered with clarity and compassion by an inventive and imaginative writer at the top of his form.

Homesick for Nowhere
Richard LeBlond

Retired field biologist Richard LeBlond has faced down a bear in Labrador, chased a spadefoot toad through the soaking undergrowth, shilled for an auction house run by men he called Laurel and Hardy, choked down home-preserved seal-ribs on the Strait of Belle Isle, and witnessed a rare performance by the leading rake-and-scrape band in the Bahamas. In short, he's has had quite a life, and he's written about it here with wit and compassion for the foibles and blessings of his fellow humans. LeBlond reveals himself as the best sort of storyteller, and an engagingly witty travel companion.

More or Less: Essays from a Year of No Buying
Susannah Q. Pratt

In 2018, Pratt and her family decided to buy nothing for a year: "We undertook a 365-day moratorium on the purchase of new clothes, toys, games, books, electronics, gear, furniture, housewares, and other things that fall in the general category of 'stuff.' For twelve months we purchased only essentials—food, toiletries, light bulbs, and a few pairs of shoes for my growing boys. We stayed out of stores and off of online shopping sites. We fixed things. We made things. We went without." The twenty-one essays in *More or Less* are much more than the story of that year. Pratt thoughtfully considers what might bring someone to step outside the usual American consumerism, coming to examine the ways in which what we buy and own can change who we are or want to be. Intertwining scenes of homelife with sustained reflection on notions of utility, disposability, and community, the book addresses the central question of how to live well in a culture of consumerism from which there is no meaningful exit.

Printed in the USA
CPSIA information can be obtained
at www.ICGtesting.com
LVHW042058090424
776893LV00001B/64